Zaner-Bloser
HANDWRITING
A Way to Self-Expression

Senior Authors

Clinton S. Hackney, Ed.D.
Language Arts Consultant

Virginia H. Lucas, Ph.D.
Professor of Education
Wittenberg University

Grade I

Contributing Authors

Janet T. Bercik, Ed.D.
Coordinator of Clinical Experiences
Northeastern Illinois University

Wilma J. Farmer, Ed.D.
Director of Elementary Education
Camden (N.J.) City School District

Gloria C. Rivera, M.A.
Former Elementary Supervisor
Zapata County (Texas) I.S.D.

Stephen E. Rogalski, B.S.
Fourth Grade Teacher
New Martinsville (W.V.) School

James A. Wilhide, Ed.D.
Former Language Arts Consultant
South Carolina State Department of Education

Consultants

Muriel E. Farley, Fairfax County (Va.) Public Schools
Janet Luttmers, Winona (Minn.) School District 861
Dianne Odell, Hickman Mills (Mo.) School District C1

Credits

Literature: "The End" from *Now We Are Six* by A. A. Milne. Copyright © 1927 by E. P. Dutton. Renewed, 1955 by A. A. Milne. Reprinted by permission of the publisher, Dutton Children's Books, A Division of Penguin Books U.S.A., Inc. "I Like to Go to School" from *The Life I Live, Collected Poems* by Lois Lenski. Copyright © 1965 by Henry Z. Walch, Inc. "Rudolph is Tired of the City" from *Bronzeville Boys and Girls* by Gwendolyn Brooks. Copyright © 1956 by Gwendolyn Brooks Blakely. Reprinted by permission of HarperCollins Publishers. "Dogs" from *Around and About* by Marchette Chute. Copyright © 1957 by E. P. Dutton, Inc. Copyright renewed 1985 by Marchette Chute. Reprinted by permission of Mary Chute Smith. "A Time for Building" from *A Song I Sang to You* by Myra Cohn Livingston. Copyright © 1984, 1969, 1967, 1965, 1959, 1958 by Myra Cohn Livingston. Reprinted by permission of Marian Reiner for the author. "Night Sky" from *In the Woods, In the Meadow, In the Sky.* New York: Scribner's, 1965. By permission of the author. "Seasons Afoot" by Beverly McLoughland. Copyright © 1987, Highlights for Children, Inc. "Saturday Night" by Lois F. Pasley from *New Poems for Children* by Carol M. Lane. Copyright © 1956.

Photos: p. 25: Regis Lefebure/Third Coast Stock Source; p. 26: Tony Casper/Third Coast Stock Source; p. 29: Jeff Smith/The Image Bank; p. 36: George R. Cassidy/Third Coast Stock Source; p. 38: Gerard Champlong/The Image Bank; p. 41: Frink/Waterhouse/H. Armstrong Roberts; p. 43: H. Armstrong Roberts; p. 50: David Phillips; p. 52: M. Elenz-Tranter/H. Armstrong Roberts; p. 53: David Joel/TSW-Click/Chicago; p. 56: James P. Rowan/TSW-Click/Chicago; p. 57: Robert Daemmrich/TSW-Click/Chicago; p. 58: Billy Barnes/Camerique/H. Armstrong Roberts; p. 62: FPG International; pp. 84, 85: NASA; p. 86: Devaney Stock Photo; p. 87: NASA; p. 89: R. Llewellyn/Superstock; p. 90: G & J Images/The Image Bank; p. 104: Kenneth Hayden/TSW-Click/Chicago; p. 105: D. Corson/H. Armstrong Roberts; p. 106: D. Muench/H. Armstrong Roberts; p. 110: H. G. Ross/H. Armstrong Roberts; p. 111: C. S. Bauer/H. Armstrong Robe[rts]; p. 114: Eric Kamp/Index Stock; p. 119: Steve Dunwell/The Im[age] Bank; p. 120: *The Velveteen Rabbit* © 1986, Random Ho[use]; p. 124: AP/Wide World; p. 125: Donald C. Johnson.

Art: Liz Allen: pp. 10, 11, 18-19, 44, 63, 108, 122; Jeni Bass[ett]: pp. 96-97, 133; Nan Brooks: pp. 14, 15, 23, 46, 47, 80-81, 115, [ ]; Rondi Colette: pp. 78, 79; Gwen Connelly: pp. 5, 6-7, 16-17, 37, 67, 68, 69, 70, 71, 72, 73, 74, 75, 76, 77, 110; Carolyn C[ ] p. 128; Lulu Delacre: pp. 39, 131; Dennis Hockerman: pp. 51, 61, 91, 92-93, 132; Karen Loccisano: pp. 12, 13, 95; Loretta Lustig: 22, 30, 60, 64-65, 100, 101, 103, 109; James Needham: pp. 40, 126, 127, 130; Stella Ormai: pp. 3, 4, 5, 28, 31, 32, 33, 34-35, 82, 98, 99, 102, 123, 129, 138-139, 140; Cathy Pavia: p. 24; Jan Pyk: p. 1[ ] Jeff Severn: pp. 27, 45, 121, 136, 137; Sally Springer: pp. 8, 9, 21, 48-49, 54-55, 59, 62, 94, 107, 111, 113, 116-117, 135, 140.

Design and production by The Quarasan Group, Inc.
Cover Photo: Aaron Haupt

ISBN 0-88085-161-9

94 95 96 97 DP 8 7 6 5 4

Table of Contents

Alphabet **3**
Tone Poem **5**

SECTION 1
**Getting Ready
For Manuscript** **6**

Basic Strokes 8
Review 14
Section Review 16

Lowercase Letters

SECTION 2
(Neighborhoods)

**Line and
Circle Letters** **18**

l i t 20
Review 23
o a d 24
Review 27

c e f 28
Review 31
Section Review 32

SECTION 3
(Animals)

More Circle Letters .. **34**

g j q 36
Review 39
u s 40
Review 42
b p 43
Review 45
Section Review 46

SECTION 4
(Health and Safety)

**Curve Forward and
Slant Line Letters** .. **48**

r n m h 50
Review 54
v y w 56
Review 59
k x z 60
Review 63
Section Review 64

Numerals

SECTION 5
(Machines and Tools)

Numerals **66**

    1 - 10 68

    Section Review 78

Uppercase Letters

SECTION 6
(World and Universe)

Line and
Circle Letters **80**

    Grouping Uppercase
      Letters 82

    L I T 84

    Review 87

    E F H 88

    Review 91

    O Q C G 92

    Review 96

    Section Review 98

SECTION 7
(Seasons)

Curve Line and
Slant Line Letters .. **100**

    P R B D 102

    Review 106

    U S J 108

    Review 111

    A N M 112

    Review 115

    Section Review 116

SECTION 8
(Creative Arts)

Slant Line Letters
Enrichment **118**

    V W Y 120

    Review 123

    K X Z 124

    Review 127

    Enrichment
      Activities 128

    Section Review 136

    Writing a Letter .. 138

Summer Fun **140**

Student Record ... **141**

Lowercase Letters

Can you name each letter?

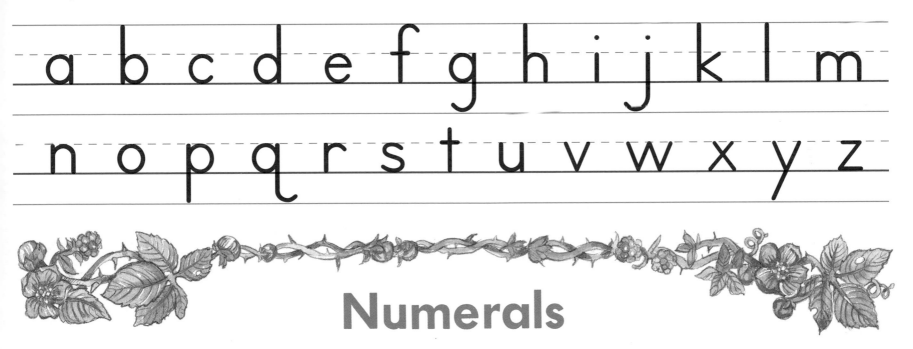

a b c d e f g h i j k l m

n o p q r s t u v w x y z

Numerals

Can you name each numeral?

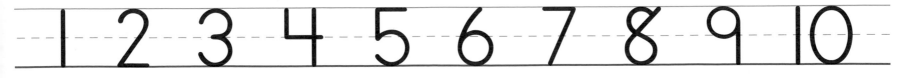

1 2 3 4 5 6 7 8 9 10

3

Can you name each letter?

A B C D E F G H I

J K L M N O P Q R

S T U V W X Y Z

When I was One,
I had just begun.

When I was Two,
I was nearly new.

When I was Three,
I was hardly Me.

When I was Four,
I was not much more.

When I was Five,
I was just alive.

But now I am Six,
I'm as clever as clever.

So I think I'll be six now
forever and ever.

A. A. Milne

My name is _____.

I am ___ years old.

Getting Ready For Manuscript

I Like to Go to School

I like to go to school,
    I want to read a book,
I want to learn the words
    And at the pictures look.

I want to learn to write,
    I like to make my name;
And when it comes recess,
    Run out to play a game.

I want to learn to count,
    Add numbers in a row;
I study hard at school,
That's where I like to go!

Lois Lenski

Top to Bottom

left hand

Paper Position

right hand

pull
down
straight

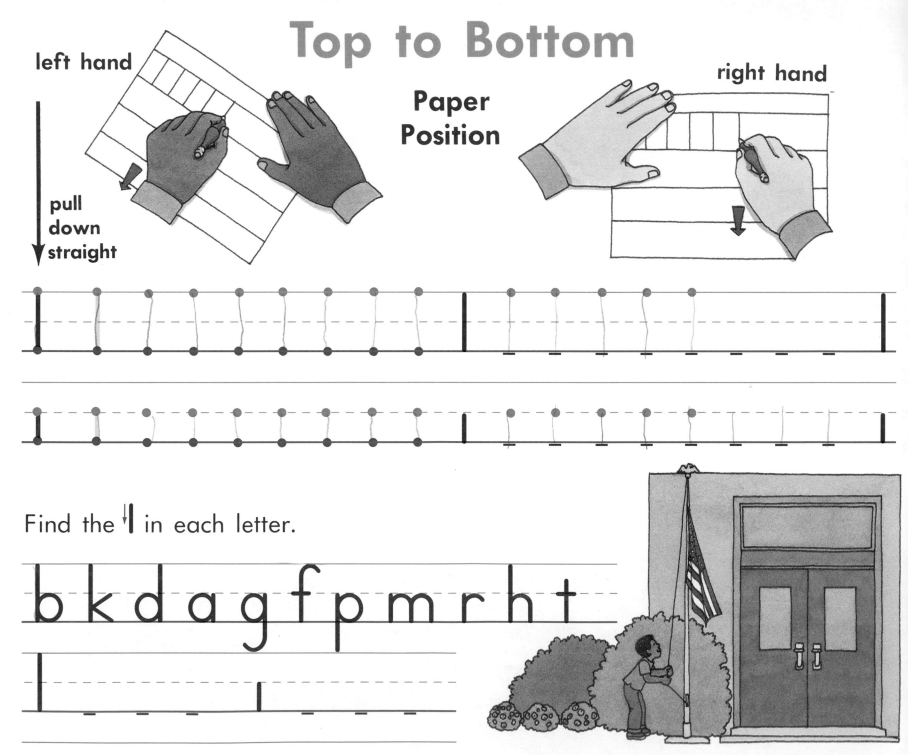

Find the ↓| in each letter.

b k d a g f p m r h t

8

Left to Right

How to Hold Your Pencil

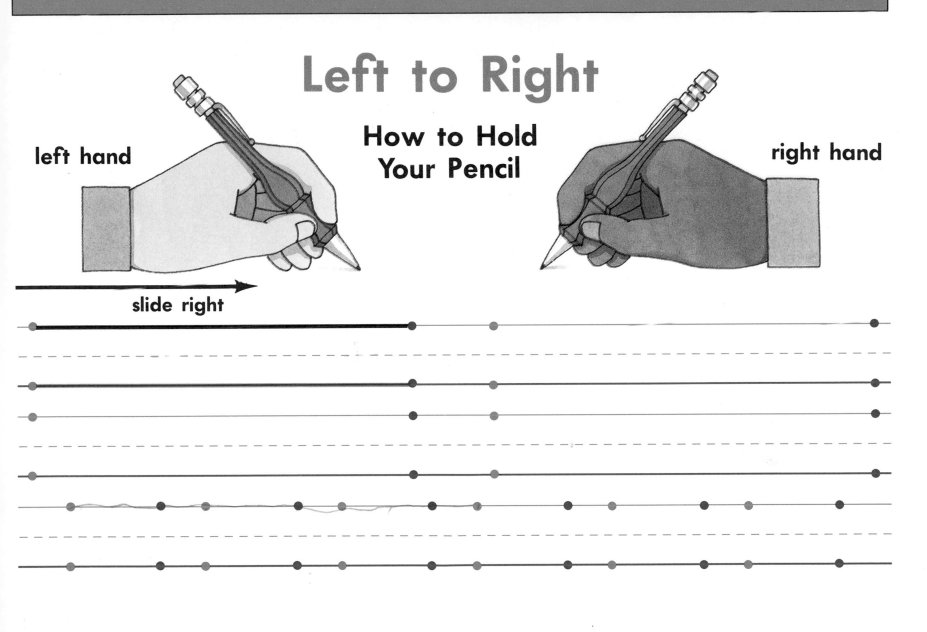

left hand

slide right

right hand

Find the ⇌ in each letter.

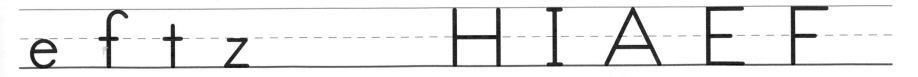

e f t z   H I A E F

Backward Circle

Find the ⟲ in each letter.

a d Q g q

Forward Circle

Find the ⟳ in each letter.

b p

How are **b** and **p** alike?   How are **b** and **p** different?

Slant Right

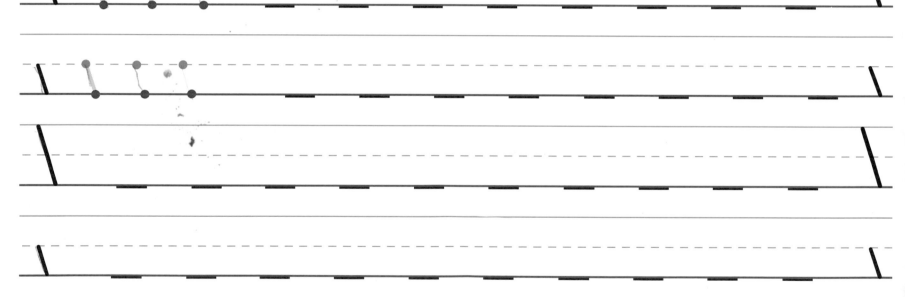

Find the 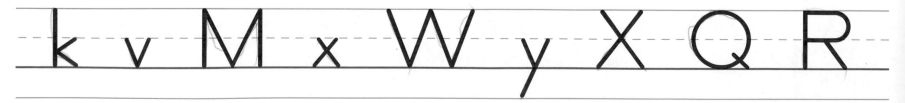 in each letter.

k v M x W y X Q R

Slant Left

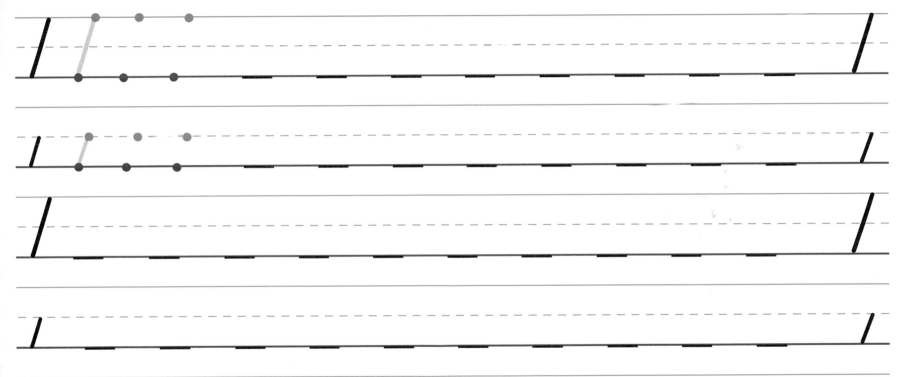

Find the / in each letter.

A k M v V w W X y Y

Basic Strokes

Trace and write the **top to bottom** strokes.

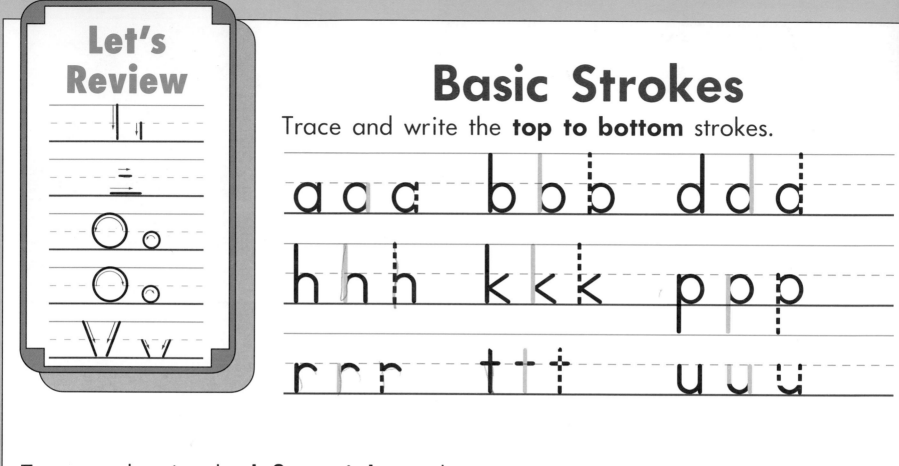

a a a   b b b   d d d

h h h   k k k   p p p

r r r   t t t   u u u

Trace and write the **left to right** strokes.

e e e   f f f   t t t   z z z

2 2 2   4 4 4   5 5 5

Trace and write the **backward circle**.

a a a   d d d   g g g   q q q

Trace and write the **forward circle**.

b b b b   p p p p   b b b b

Trace and write the **slant strokes**.

v v v v   y y y y   w w w w

x x x x   z z z z   k k k k

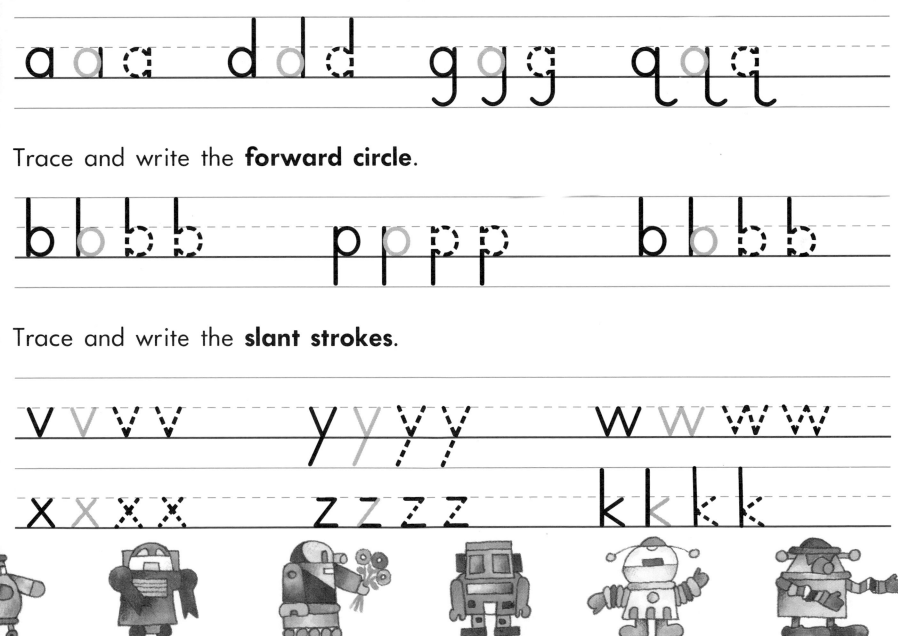

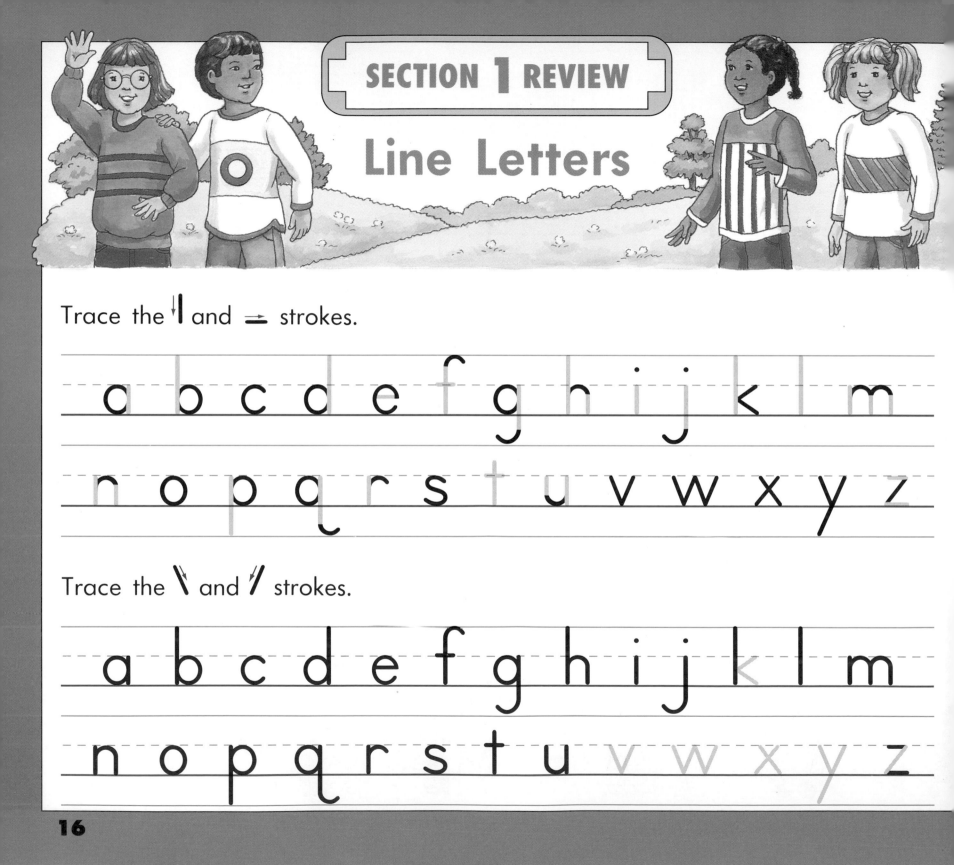

Trace the | and ⇌ strokes.

a b c d e f g h i j k l m

n o p q r s t u v w x y z

Trace the \ and / strokes.

a b c d e f g h i j k l m

n o p q r s t u v w x y z

Circle Letters

Trace the O.

a b c d e f g h i j k l m
n o p q r s t u v w x y z

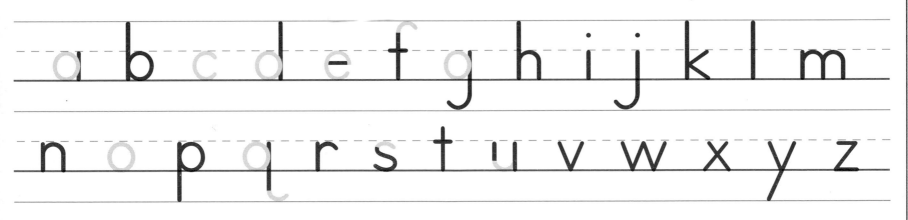

Trace the O.

a b c d e f g h i j k l m
n o p q r s t u v w x y z

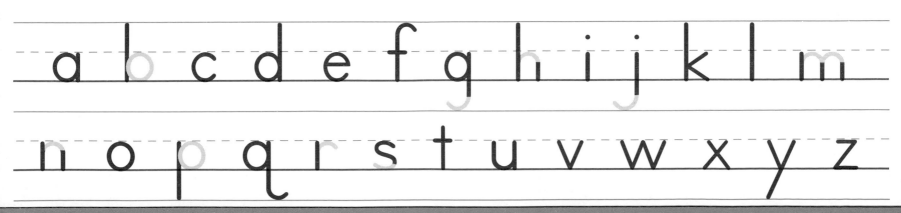

LOWERCASE
Line and Circle Letters

Rudolph Is Tired of the City

These buildings are too close to me.
I'd like to PUSH away.
I'd like to live in the country.
And spread my arms all day.

I'd like to spread my breath out, too
As farmers' sons and daughters do.

I'd tend the cows and chickens.
I'd do the other chores.
Then, all the hours left I'd go
A-SPREADING out-of-doors.

Gwendolyn Brooks

Trace and write.

live ___ive ___ive ___ive

all a___ a___ a___

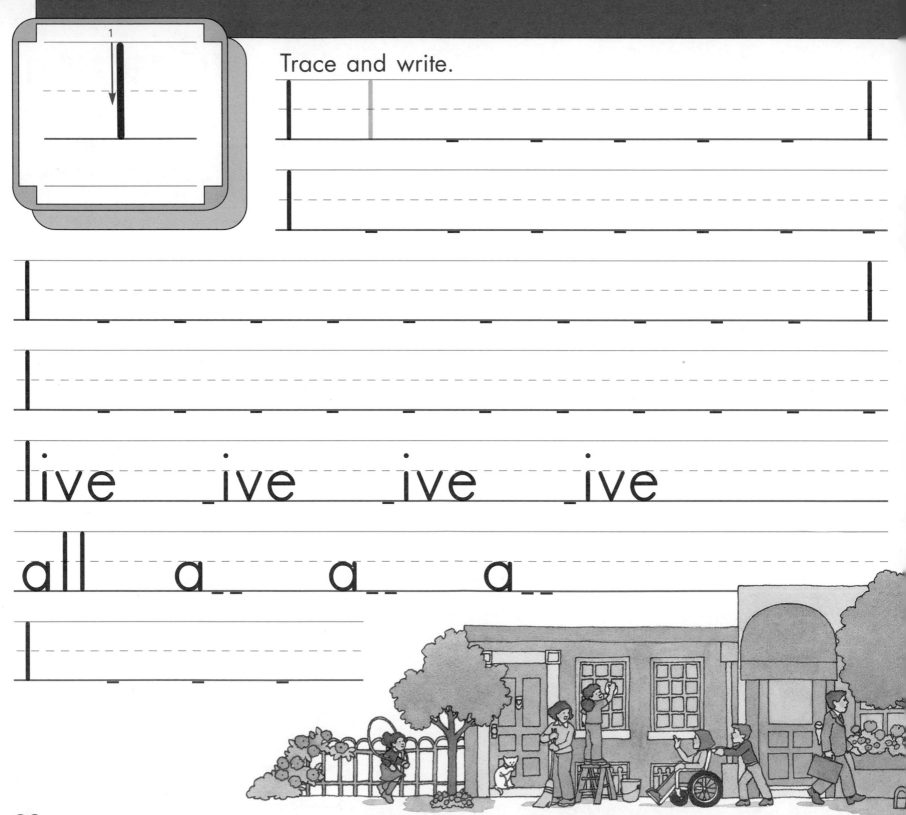

Trace and write.

i · · · · · · · · · · · · · i

i · · · · · · · · · · · · ·

i · · · · · · · · · · · · · i

i · · · · · · · · · · · · ·

in   _n   _n   _n

inside   _ns_de

i   _

Trace and write.

t   t   — — — — — —   t

t — — — — — — — — —

t — — — — — — — — — — — — t

t — — — — — — — — — — — — —

little   ___e   ___e

town   _own   _own

t — — — — —

Write a sentence describing where you live.

22

Let's Review

l i t

l _____ l

i _____ i

t _____ t

clean   c_ean

litter   ___er   ___er

l _____ i _____

t _____

23

Trace and write.

O   O   O

O   O

O

lot

Go home.

G_ h_me_

a

a a _ _ _ _ _ _ _ a

a _ _ _ _ _ _ _ _

a _ _ _ _ _ _ _ a

a _ _ _ _ _ _

ball b _ _ b _

Play ball.

P_y b_

a _ _ _

25

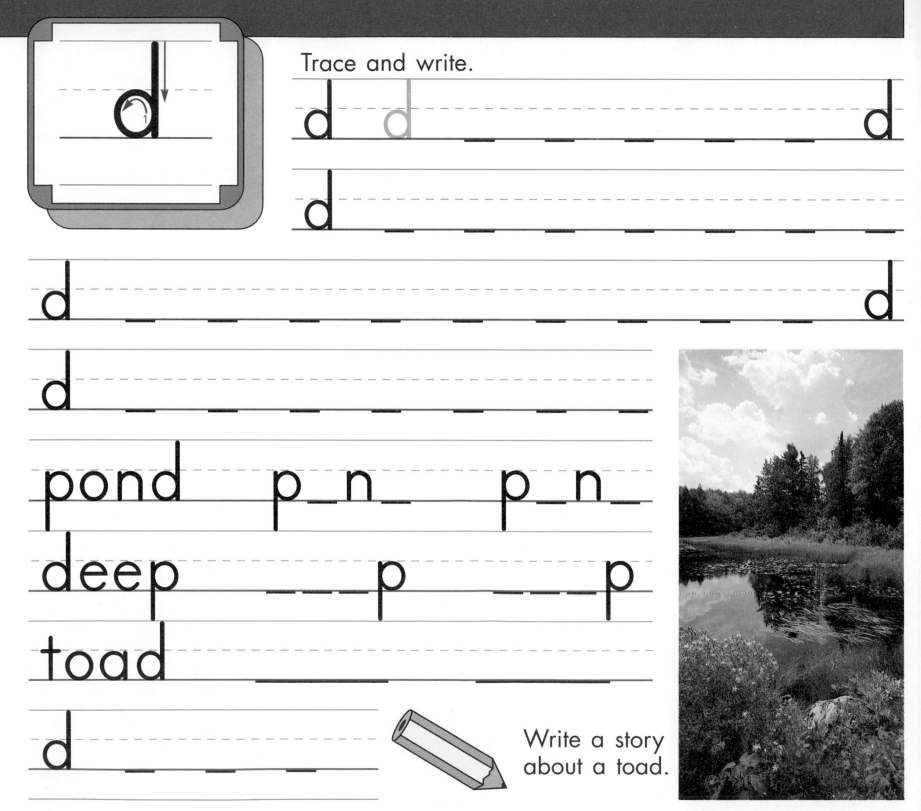

Trace and write.

d   d   d

d

d   d

d

pond   p _ n   p _ n

deep   p   p

toad

d

Write a story
about a toad.

26

o a d

Maple Drive

Pine Avenue

Oak Road

Elm Street

o _ _ _ _ _

a _ _ _ _ _

d _ _ _ _ _

road r _ _ _ r _ _ _

old road _ _ _ r _ _ _

o _ _ _ a _ _ _ d _ _ _

Trace and write.

C   c   c   _ _ _ _ _ _   c

c   _ _ _ _ _ _ _ _

c   _ _ _ _ _ _ _ _   c

c   _ _ _ _ _ _ _

city   _ _ y   _ _ y

country   _ _ un _ ry   _ _ un _ ry

mice   m _ _ e   m _ _ e   m _ _ e

c _ _ _ _

28

e _e_ — — — — — — e

e — — — — — — — — —

e — — — — — — — e

e — — — — — — — —

store s _ r _

sale s _ _ s _ _ s _ _

ride r _ _ r _ _ r _ _

e — — — —

Write about a trip to the store.

29

f

f f f

f

f f

farm ___rm ___rm

calf

field

fox ___x ___x

f

c _ _ _ _ _

e _ _ _ _

f _ _ _ _

city _ _ y _ _ y _ _ y

mouse m_us_ m_us_

friend _ r_n_ _ r_n_

c _ _ _ _ e _ _ _ _

f _ _ _ _

Find these hidden pictures and complete each word.

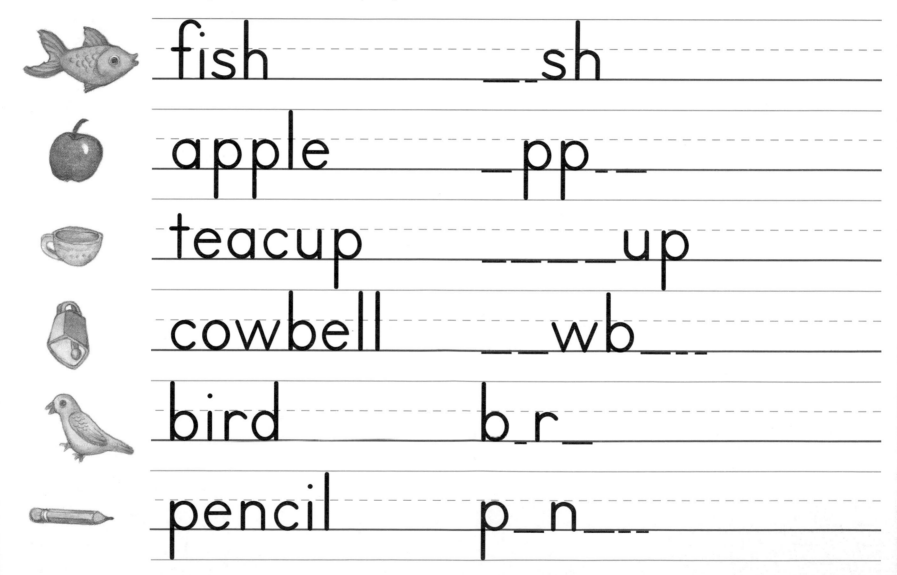

fish   __sh

apple   _pp__

teacup   ___up

cowbell   __wb___

bird   b_r_

pencil   p_n___

Can you find other objects?

City Mouse and Country Mouse

o _ _ a _ _ d _ _

c _ _ e _ _ f _ _

More Circle Letters

Dogs

The dogs I know
Have many shapes.
For some are big and tall,

And some are long,

And
some
are thin,

And some are fat and small.

And some are little bits of fluff
And have no shape at all.

Marchette Gaylord Chute

g

Trace and write.

g g — — — — — — — — g

g — — —

g — — — — — — — — — g

g — — — —

goat ——————— ———

dog ——— ———

geese — — s —

g — — — —

Trace and write.

j j j — — — — — — — j

j — — — — — — — — — —

j — — — — — — — — — — j

j — — — — — — — — — —

jungle _un_____

just _us_ _us_

join ___n ___n

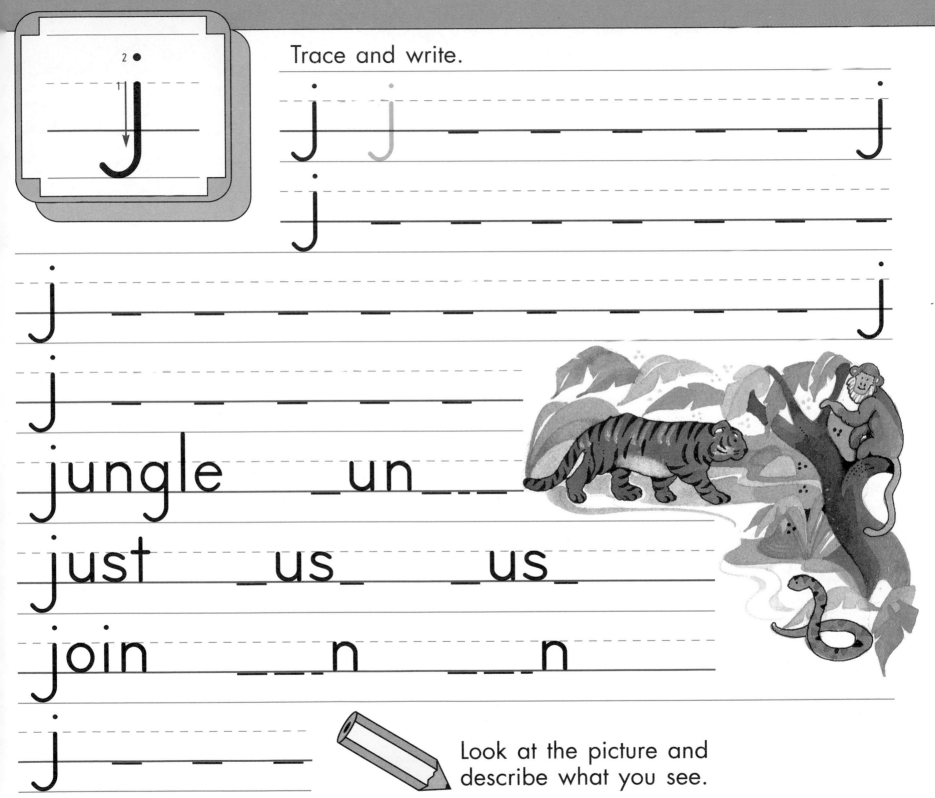

j — — — — —

Look at the picture and describe what you see.

37

q q _ _ _ _ _ _ _ q

q _ _ _ _ _ _ _ _

q _ _ _ _ _ _ _ q

q _ _ _ _ _ _ _

quiet _u_ _ _

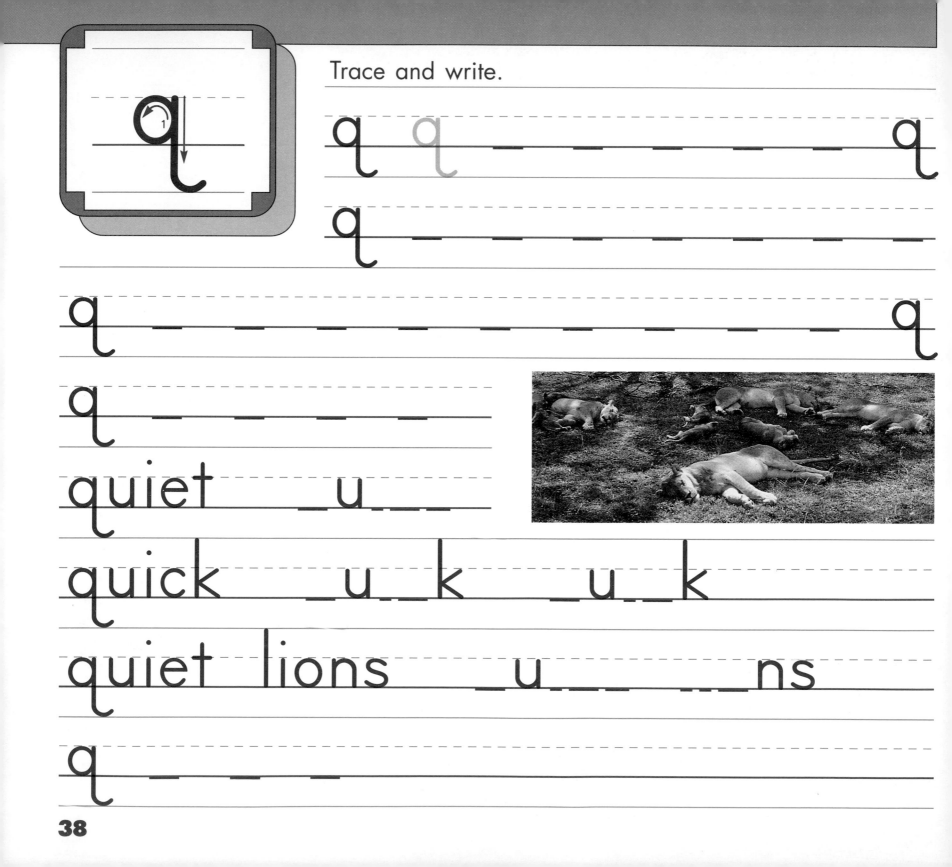

quick _u_ k _u_ k

quiet lions _u_ _ _ ns

q _ _ _ _ _ _ _

g — — — — j — — —

q — — — —

pigs dig

p _ _ s _ _ _

squirrels whirl

s _ u r r _ s wh _ r _

dogs jog

_ _ _ s _ _ _

u

u u u

u

u

u

bugs b_s b_s

under _n_r

ground _r_n

u

40

s

s s s   s

s

s   s

s

fish   h   h

seals

sea

s

Write a story about an
animal that lives in the sea.

41

Let's Review

u s

duck   fish

sheep   skunk

seal   squirrel

Write the letters.

u ___ ___ ___   s ___ ___ ___

Land Animals

_ h _ p

_ _ _ rr _

_ k _ nk

Water Animals

_ _ _ _

_ _ _ k

_ _ h

b b   b

b

b   b

baby birds   y   r

? ?   ?

What do birds eat?

Wh   r

b   ?

p p p p

p

p p

pig

puddle

The pig is in a puddle.

Th____n_____

p

44

Let's Review

b p

Write the letters.

b _ _ _ p _ _ _

Match mother to baby.

bear· ·tadpole

frog· ·cub

dog· ·pup

Write the names of the baby animals.

1. _____

2. _____

3. _____

Checkpoint
Are your ◯ round? ☐ Yes ☐ No

45

1. What rhymes with  bat?

_____

- - - - - - - - - - - - -

_____

2. What rhymes with log?

_____

- - - - - - - - - - - - -

_____

3. What rhymes with heel?

_____

- - - - - - - - - - - - -

_____

fan   cat

dog   sun

horse   seal

4. What rhymes with 🎩 lid?

_____

- - - - - - - - - - - - -

_____

lake

squid

5. What rhymes with 🛁 tub?

_____

- - - - - - - - - - - - -

_____

cub

boat

6. What rhymes with 🪏 dig?

_____

- - - - - - - - - - - - -

_____

tiger

pig

Curve Forward and Slant Line Letters

Safety

Stop! Look! Listen, Jim!
Before you cross the street.
Use your eyes and ears
Before you use your feet.

Unknown

9102

Trace and write.

r   r   — — — —   r

r   — — — — — — —

r   — — — — — — —   r

fire   — — — —

rescue   — —

The fire alarm rang.

T — — — — m — n —

r — — —

Explain what you do when
the fire alarm rings at school.

50

Trace and write.

n   n   n

n

n   n

danger

!   !

No running!

N

n   !

No Running

51

m   m   m

m

m   m

meal

meat

Please pour my milk.

P_____y___k

m_____

Write a list of good foods you
would use to plan a meal.

h

Trace and write.

h   h _ _ _ _ _ _   h

h _ _ _ _ _ _ _ _

h _ _ _ _ _ _ _ _   h

health _ _ _ _ _ _

helper _ _ _ _ _

She helps him.

S

h _ _ _

r n m h

r _____

n _____

m _____

h _____

doctor
hospital
mask
nurse

Use the words in the box to complete each sentence.

1. A nice person took me to a _____.

2. I went to the _____ when I broke my arm.

3. There was a friendly _____ who smiled at me.

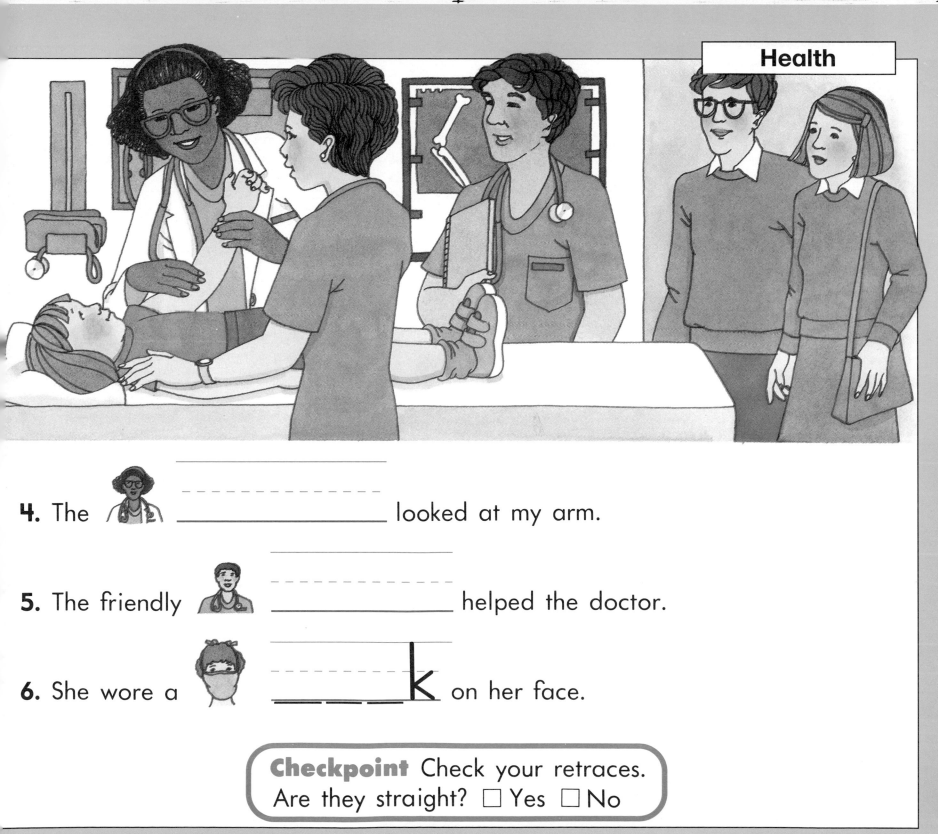

4. The <u>   </u> looked at my arm.

5. The friendly <u>   </u> helped the doctor.

6. She wore a <u>   </u>k on her face.

Checkpoint Check your retraces.
Are they straight? ☐ Yes ☐ No

V

V   V   v

V

v   v

dive

river

Never dive into a river.

N

V

56

Trace and write.

y y _ _ _ _ _ _ _ _ _ _ _ _ y

y _

y _ y

play _ _ _ _ _ _ _ _ _ _ _ _ _ _ _ _ _

safely _ _ _ _ _ _ _ _ _ _ _ _ _

Do you play safely?

D _

y _ _ _ _ _ _ _

Explain how to play
your favorite game.

57

W W   W

W

w   w

wait

watch

work   k   k

road work   k

W

58

Let's Review

v y w

v ___ ___ ___ y ___ ___ ___

w ___ ___ ___ ___

School Safety

Wait your turn.

W

Never push or shove.

N

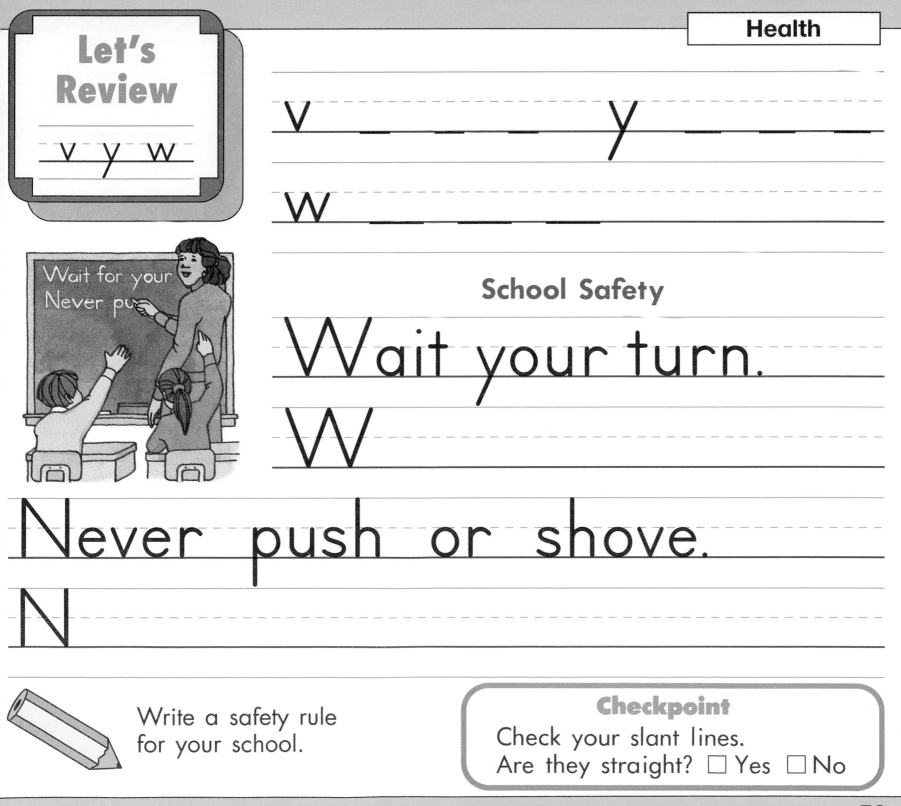

Write a safety rule for your school.

Checkpoint
Check your slant lines.
Are they straight? ☐ Yes ☐ No

59

k   k   k

k

k   k

kicks _____ _____

kickball _____

Niki kicks the ball.

N

k

X X   X

X

x

exercise

extra

Alex did exercises.

A

x

Z   z

Z

Z   Z

pizza

Do you like pizza?

D

Z

Paper Position

left hand

right hand

Let's Review

k x z

Write the letters and words.

k

x   z

Ants on a Log
celery stalk
peanut butter
raisins

Wash and dry the celery. Cut it crosswise into two or three-inch pieces. Fill each piece with peanut butter, and put a few raisins on the top of each piece.

Healthful Snacks

cereal mix

pizza

milk

Checkpoint
Are the lines in your letters smooth? ☐ Yes ☐ No

63

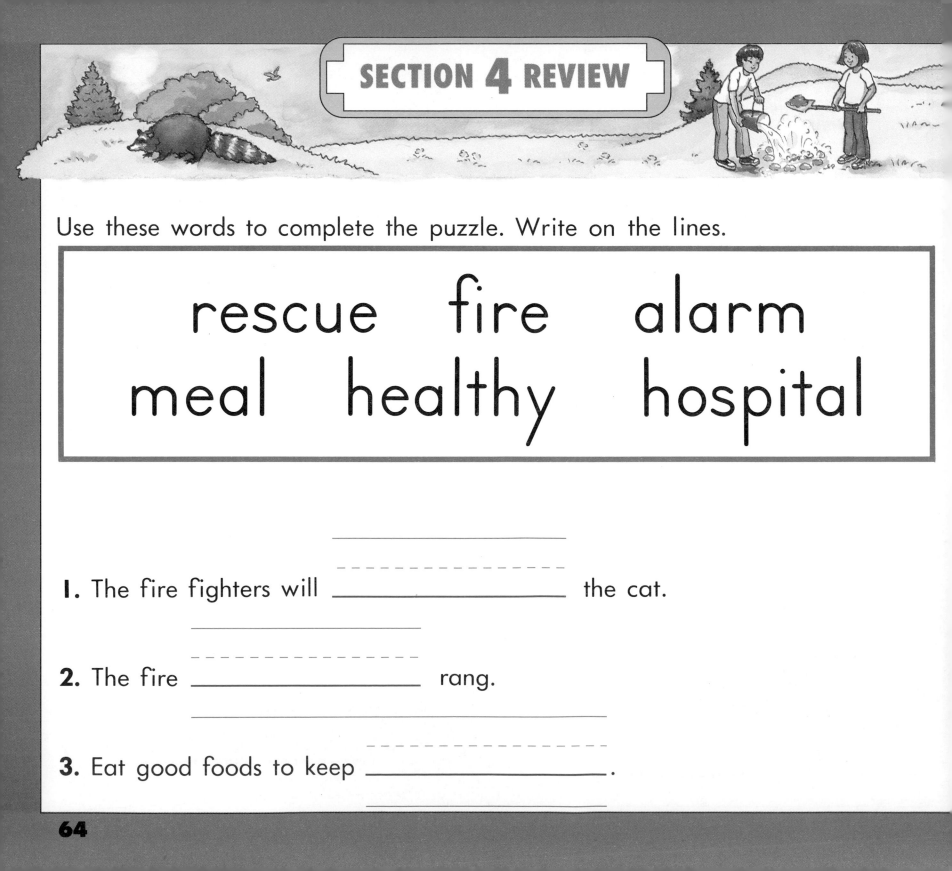

Use these words to complete the puzzle. Write on the lines.

rescue   fire   alarm

meal   healthy   hospital

1. The fire fighters will _____ the cat.

2. The fire _____ rang.

3. Eat good foods to keep _____.

1. ☐e☐c☐e   4. ☐os☐ital

2. ala☐☐   5. fi☐e

3. ☐ealt☐y   6. ☐eal

4. Dr. Smith works in a _____.

5. The campers made sure the _____ was out.

6. We ate a good _____ at noon.

Numerals

A Time for Building

A dozen machines
come roaring down,
tractors and shovels,
hydraulics and dumps,
mixers and graders,
diggers and pumps,

pushing and groaning and moving the road
to another place in town.

Myra Cohn Livingston

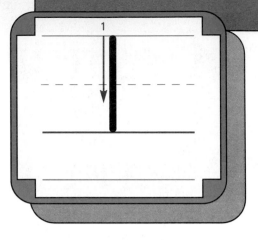

Let's Build a Clubhouse!

Trace and write.

I   I

I

I

one _____ done _____

I girl _____

I boy _____

I

One clubhouse when we are done

2

Trace and write.

2 2 _ _ _ 2

2 _ _ _

2 _ _ _ 2

two _ _ new _ _

2 wagons _ _ _

2 _ _ _

Two wagons shiny and new

3

Trace and write.

3 3 _ _ _ _ _ _ _ _ 3

3 _ _ _ _ _ _ _

3 _ _ _ _ _ _ _ _ 3

three _ _ _ _ _ _

tree _ _ _ _ _

3 buckets _ _ _

3 _ _ _ _ _

Three paint buckets by the tree

70

4

Trace and write.

4 4 4   4

4

4   4

four   door

4 hammers

4

4

Four hammers to build the door

Trace and write.

5 5 5 5

5

5 5

five   drive

5 shovels

Five shovels to dig the drive

5

72

6

6 6   6

6

6   6

six   bricks

6 brushes

6

Six brushes to paint the bricks

7

Trace and write.

7 7 7

7

7

7

seven   Kevin K

7 levers

7

Seven levers to help Kevin

8

8 8   8

8

8   8

eight   gate

8   8

8

Eight screws to hinge the gate

9

Trace and write.

9   9   9

9

9   9

nine   sign

9 letters

9

Nine letters in the sign

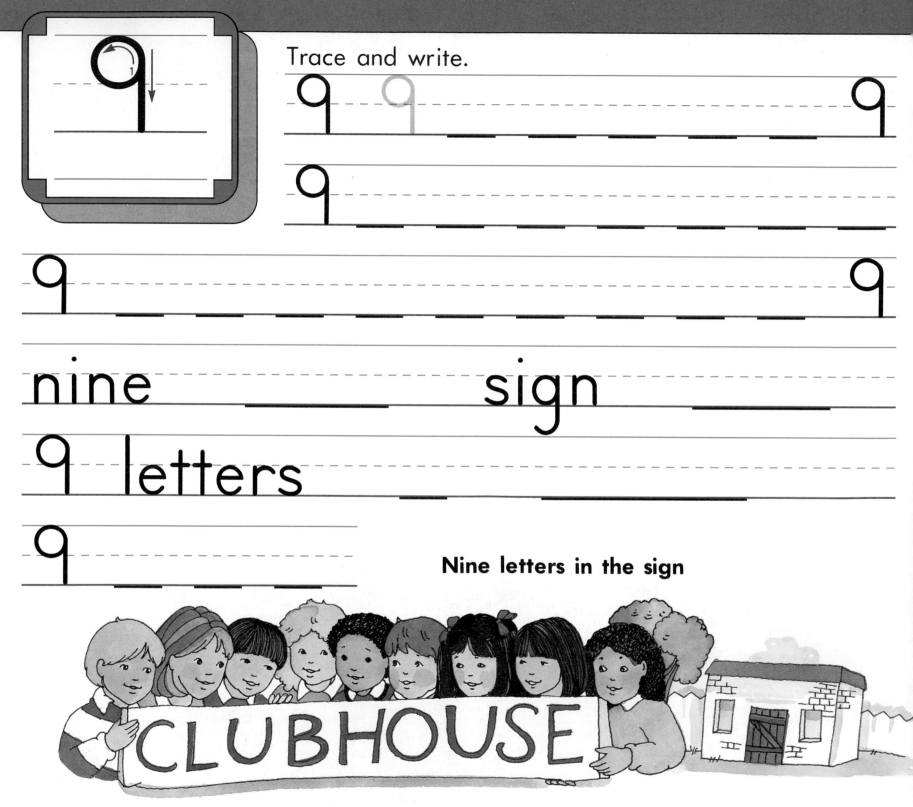

CLUBHOUSE

10

Trace and write.

10 10   10

10

10   10

ten   Ben   B

10

Gwen, Ben, and the others make 10.

77

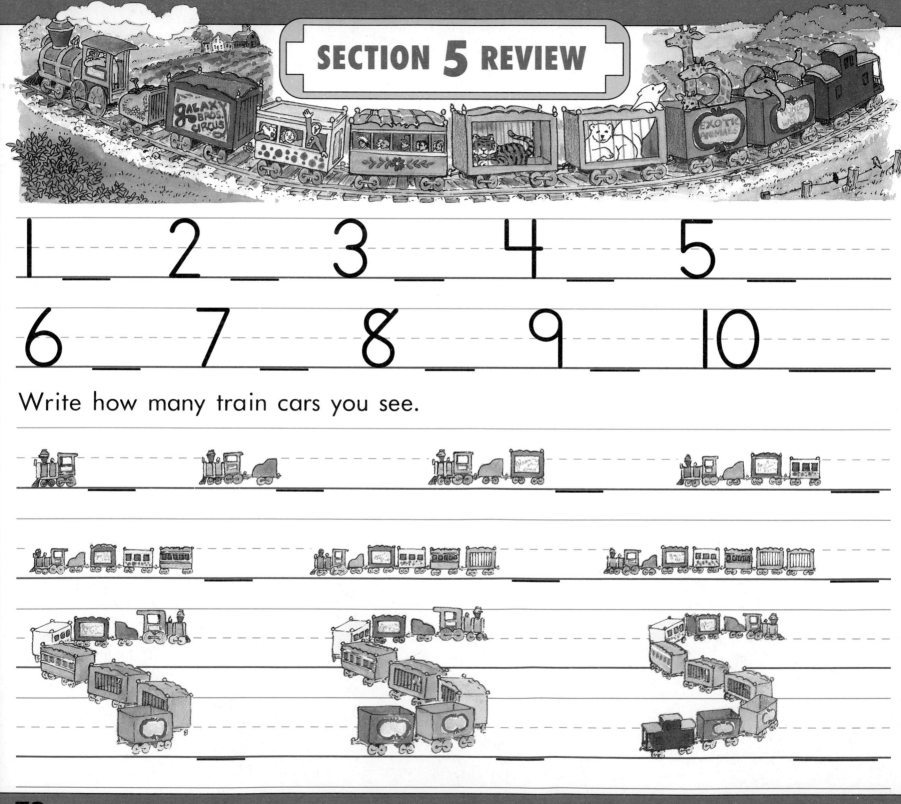

1   2   3   4   5

6   7   8   9   10

Write how many train cars you see.

Write how many you see in the picture above.

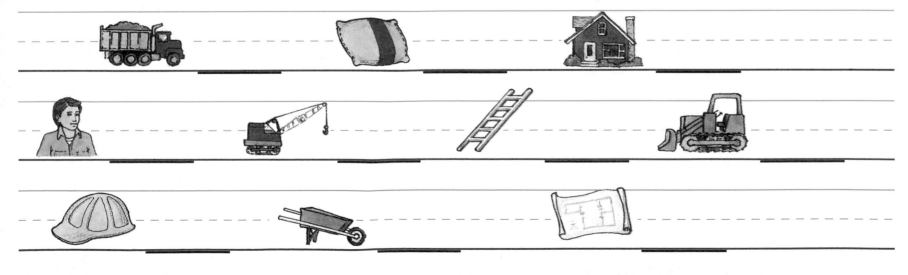

UPPERCASE
Line and Circle Letters

Night Sky

The sky looks bigger
by night than day,
with so many stars
so far away.

Aileen Fisher

Uppercase Letters

Which letter has 4 straight lines?

E F H I L T

Which letters have a complete circle?

C G O Q

Which letters have no slant line?   Which letter has no straight line?

B D P R   J S U

Which letter has four slant strokes?

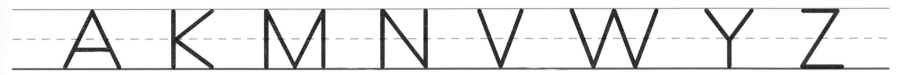

A K M N V W Y Z

Match the uppercase letter to the lowercase letter.

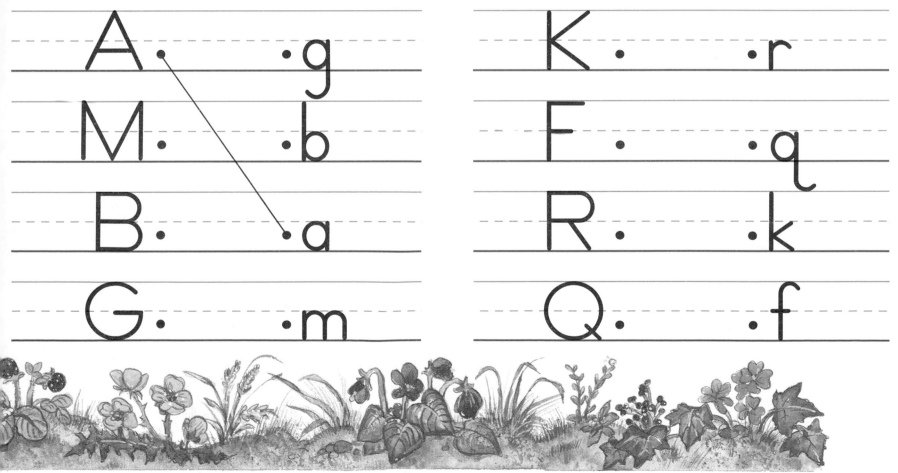

A .   . g

M .   . b

B .   . a

G .   . m

K .   . r

F .   . q

R .   . k

Q .   . f

Trace and write.

L   L   L

L

L   L

Larry

Lift off!

Linda watched.

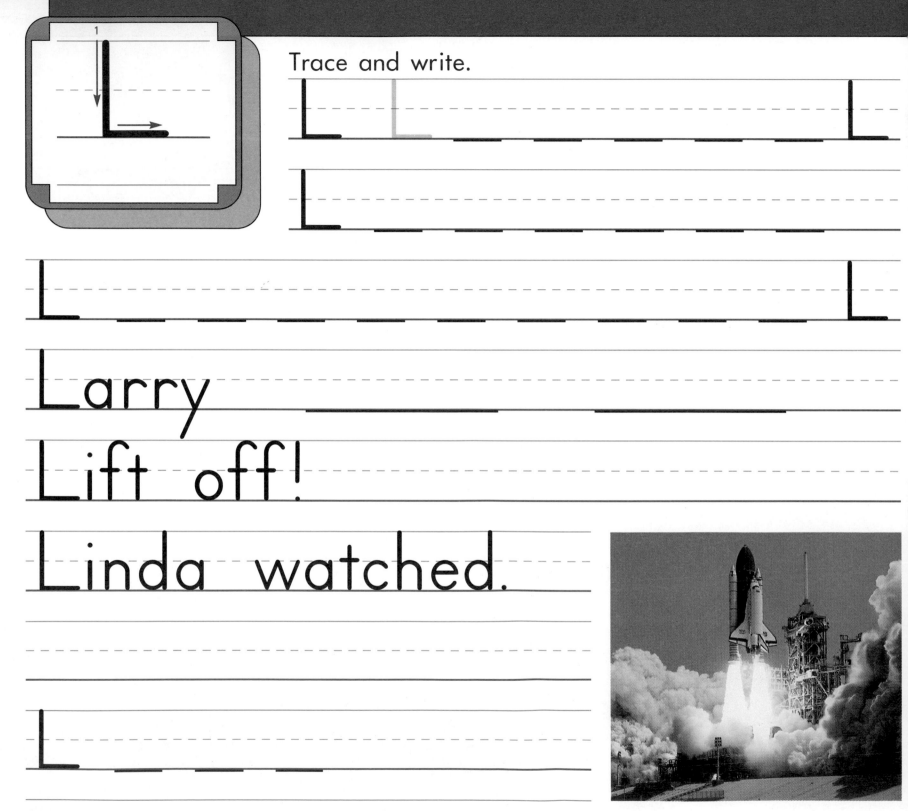

L

Trace and write.

I I I

I

" "   " "   " "

"I see the earth."

"I see bright lights."

I   " "

85

T T T

T

T

Tim and Ted are pilots.

Traci

T

Write why you would or
would not want to be a pilot.

Let's Review
L I T

The Landing

I see the shuttle.

The wheels are down.

Touch down!

Trace and write.

E   E   E   E

E

E   E

Earth

Lake Erie

Ed sails with Eric.

E

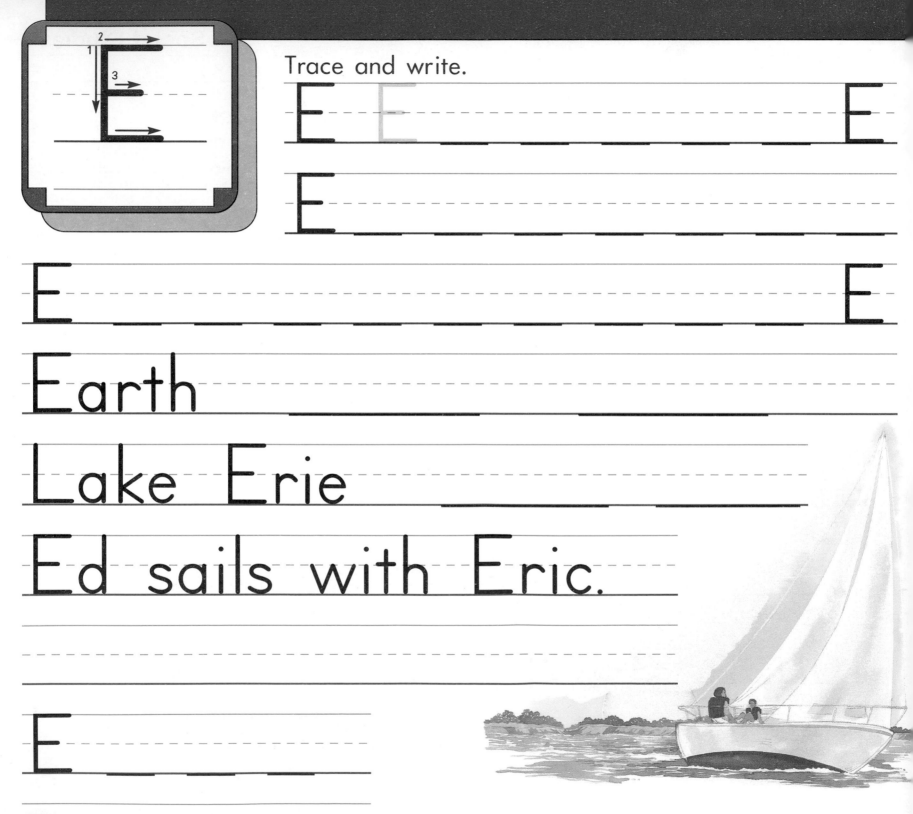

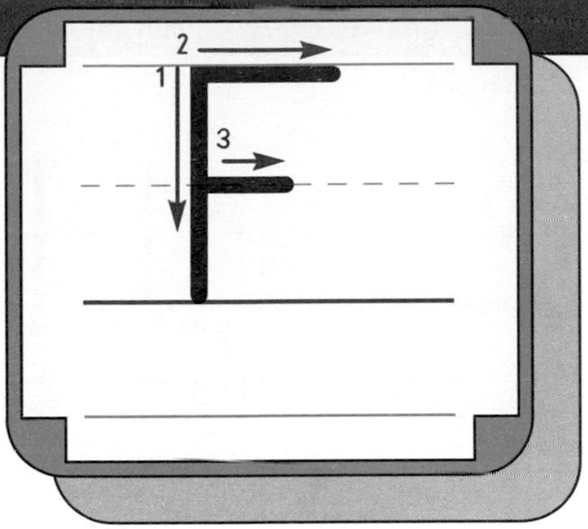

F

Trace and write.

F F F

F

F F

Florida

Felipe

Fran swims in Florida.

F

Trace and write.

H H H H

H

H H

Heiki

Hawaii

Henry surfs in Hawaii.

H

Let's Review

E F H

Freda

Edward

Finland

England

Holland

Heidi

Edward lives in England.
Freda lives in Finland.
Heidi lives in Holland.

Write the children's names.

Write where each child lives.

Write a story about
Edward, Freda, and Heidi.

Checkpoint
Check to see that your letters
are wide enough.

Trace and write.

Oz

Over the rainbow

Once upon a time

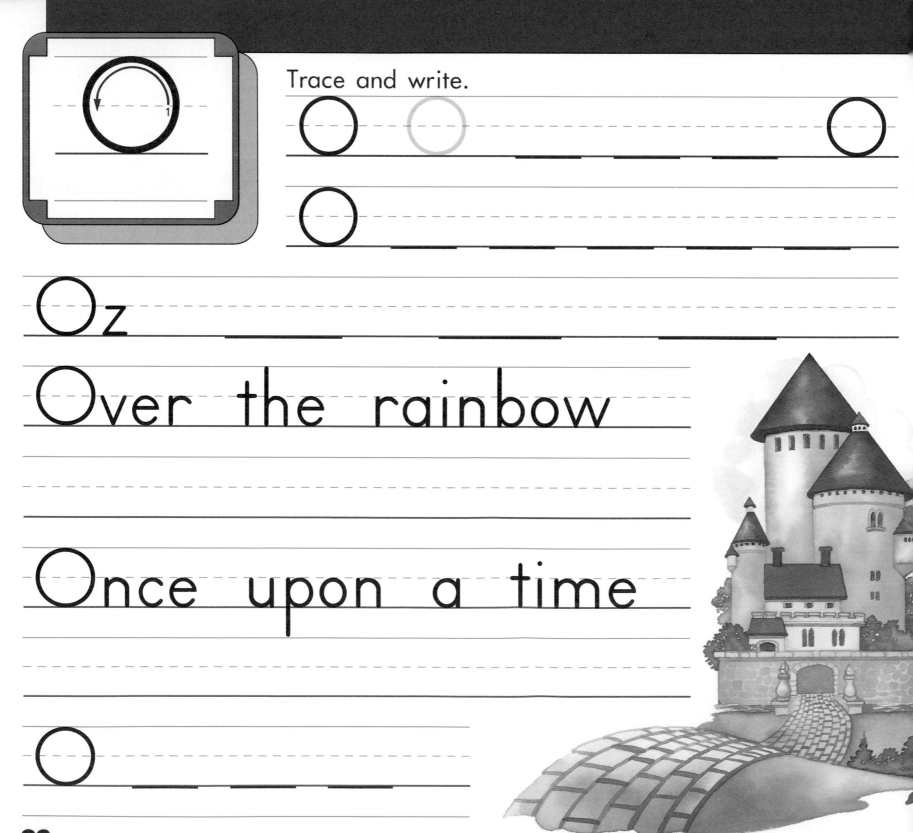

Trace and write.

Q Q Q ___ ___ ___ Q

Q ___ ___ ___

, ___ ___ ___ ___ ___ ,

Quick, Quinn, look at the rainbow!

Q ___ ___ ___ , ___ ___

Trace and write.

C C C   C

C

C   C

Carrots

Corn

Carlos grows cabbage.

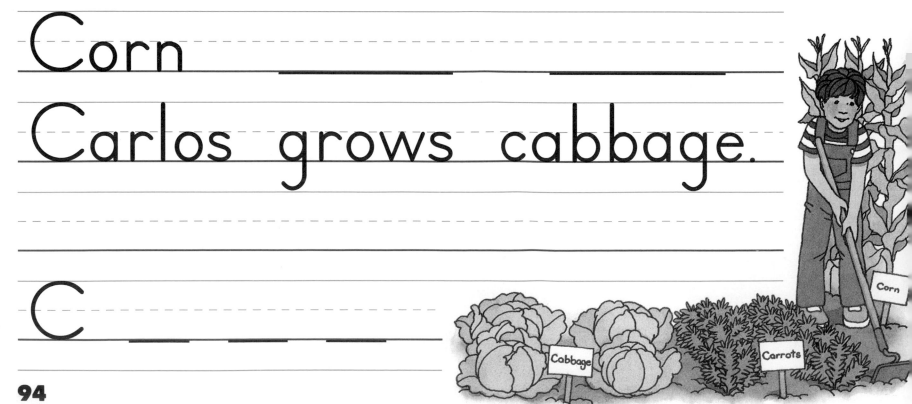

C

94

Trace and write.

G G G   G

G

G   G

Gloria

Gail's Grocery

G

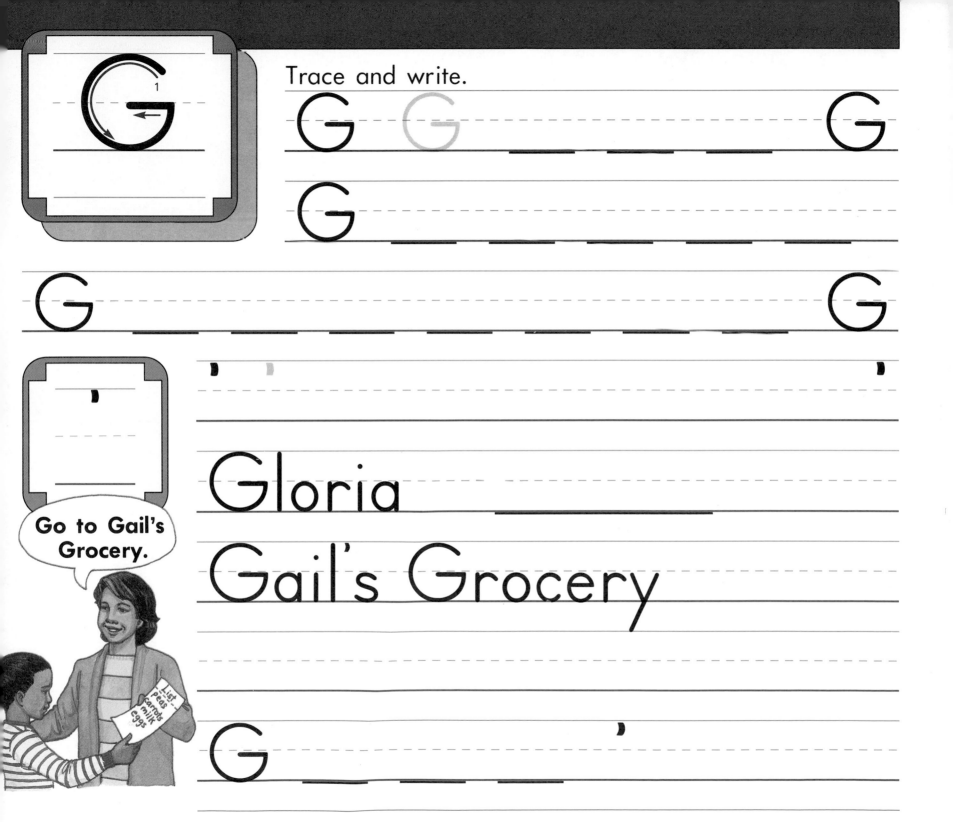

Go to Gail's Grocery.

Clouds

Have you ever stopped to look
At clouds up in the sky?
They look like animals
Going by.

John Harton, Age 10

Cow

O ___ ___ ___ ___ ___

Q ___ ___ ___ ___

C ___ ___ ___ ___

G ___ ___ ___ ___

Write the six words that name the pictures in the clouds.

1. _____

2. _____

3. _____

4. _____

5. _____

6. _____

Owl

Goose

Goat

Queen

Cat

My Poem About Clouds

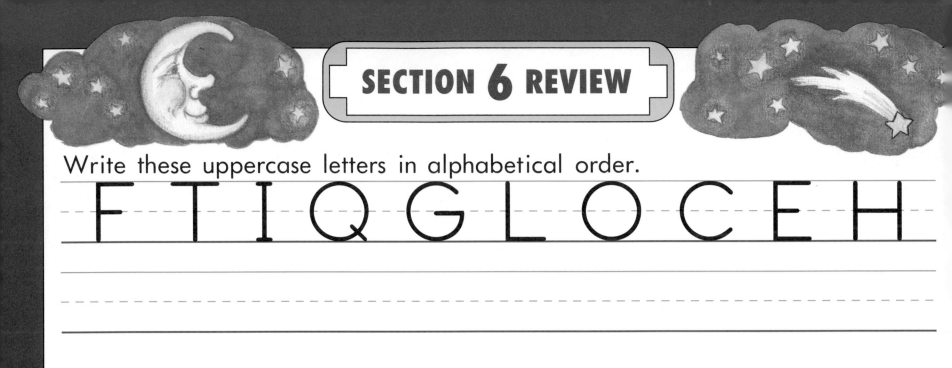

Write these uppercase letters in alphabetical order.

F T I Q G L O C E H

Use these letters to write the answers below.

1. Write a letter that has three strokes.

2. Which letter is closest to the end of the alphabet? Write it.

3. Write a letter that has only one stroke.

4. Write the letter that has four strokes.

Star light, star bright,
First star I see tonight,
I wish I may, I wish I might
Have the wish I wish tonight.

Write your own poem.

Curve and Slant Line Letters

Seasons Afoot

Spring wheels in
On roller skates,
Zooms up and down
The street.

Winter plods in
Heavily
With snow-boots
On its feet.

Summer jumps in
Barefoot,
Kicking water
In the pool.

Autumn squeaks
In brand-new shoes—
Nervously, to
School.

Beverly McLoughland

Trace and write.

P   P   P   P

P

P   P

Pilgrims

Peter

Peter gathered pumpkins.

P

Trace and write.

R R R _ _ _ _ R

R

R R

Rudolph

Reindeer

Red River

R

Trace and write.

B B B _ _ _ _ B

B _ _ _ _ _ _

B _ _ _ _ _ _ B

Butterflies flutter.

Birds can fly fast.

B _ _ _ _

Write about things that fly.

104

D

Trace and write.

D D D D

D

D D

Dandelions and Daisies

Deb picks flowers.

D

Dig in sand.

Pick up shells.

Drive down Beach Road.

Run in the sun.

Checkpoint
Do your letters **R** and **B** have a good **P** in them? ☐ Yes ☐ No

P ― ― ― R ― ―

B ― ― ― D ― ―

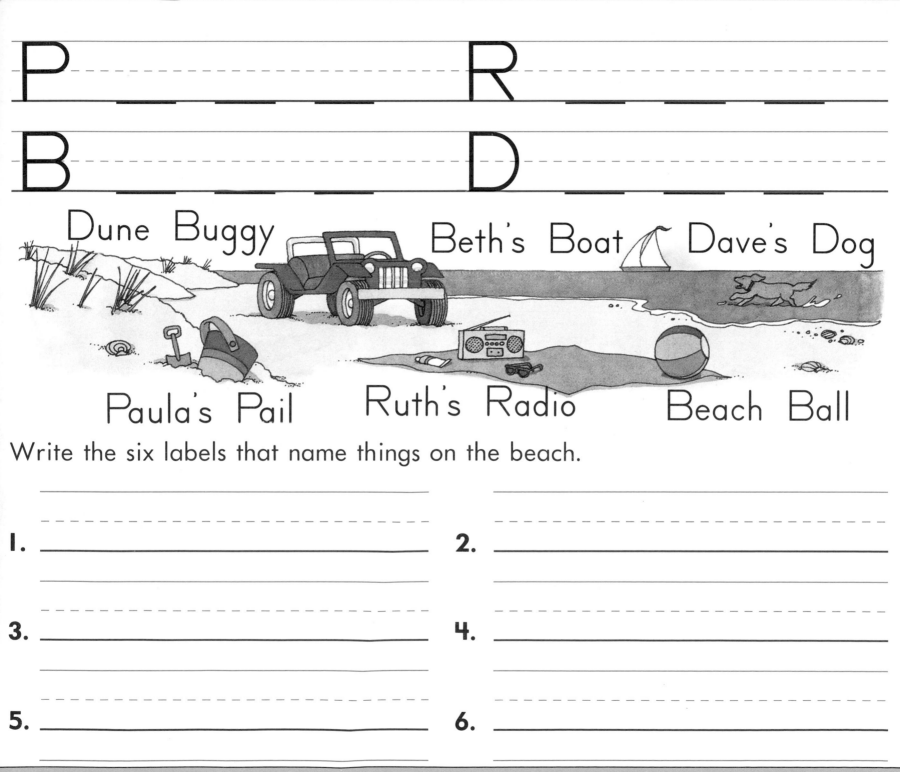

Dune Buggy

Beth's Boat   Dave's Dog

Paula's Pail   Ruth's Radio   Beach Ball

Write the six labels that name things on the beach.

1. _____

2. _____

3. _____

4. _____

5. _____

6. _____

U

Trace and write.

U U   U   U U

U U

U U

Umbrella down!

Umbrella up!

U U

108

S

S S S   S

S

S   S

Spring

Summer

Sing about the seasons.

S

109

Trace and write.

J   J   J   J

J

J   J

June 14

July 4

July 4 is a holiday.

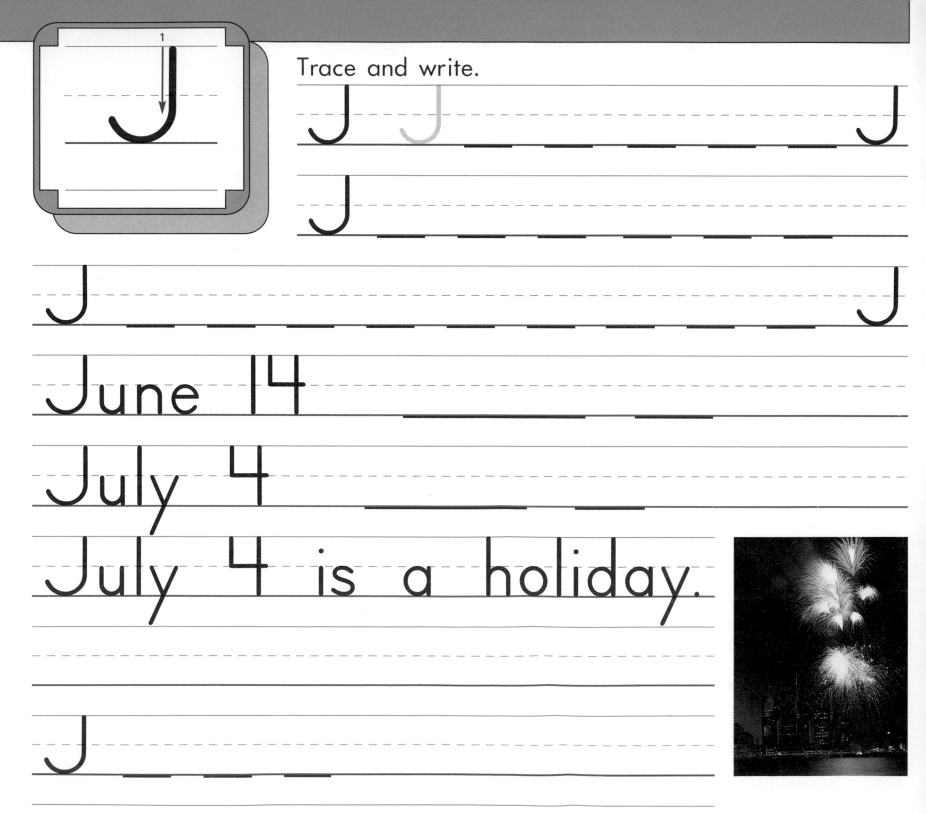

J

110

Let's Review

U S J

U _ _ _ _ _   S _ _ _ _ _

J _ _ _ _

United States

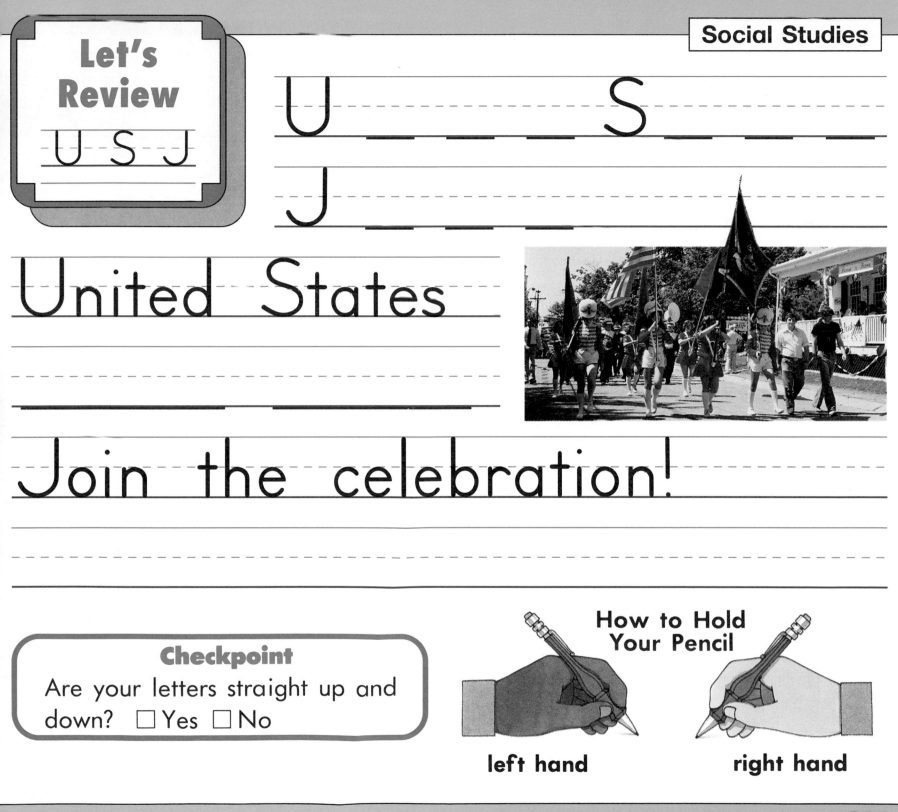

Join the celebration!

Checkpoint

Are your letters straight up and down? ☐ Yes ☐ No

How to Hold Your Pencil

left hand   right hand

A

Trace and write.

A A A _____ _____ _____ A

A _____ _____ _____

A _____ _____ _____ A

Autumn leaves fall.

Andy rakes leaves.

A _____

N

1 2

Trace and write.

N   N   N   N

N

N   N

Nights are longer
in November.

N

Describe the
night sky.

M

1 2

Trace and write.

M   M   _ _ _ _ _   M

M   _ _ _ _ _ _ _

M   _ _ _ _ _ _ _ _ _   M

March _____

Maine _____

March is windy.

M _ _ _

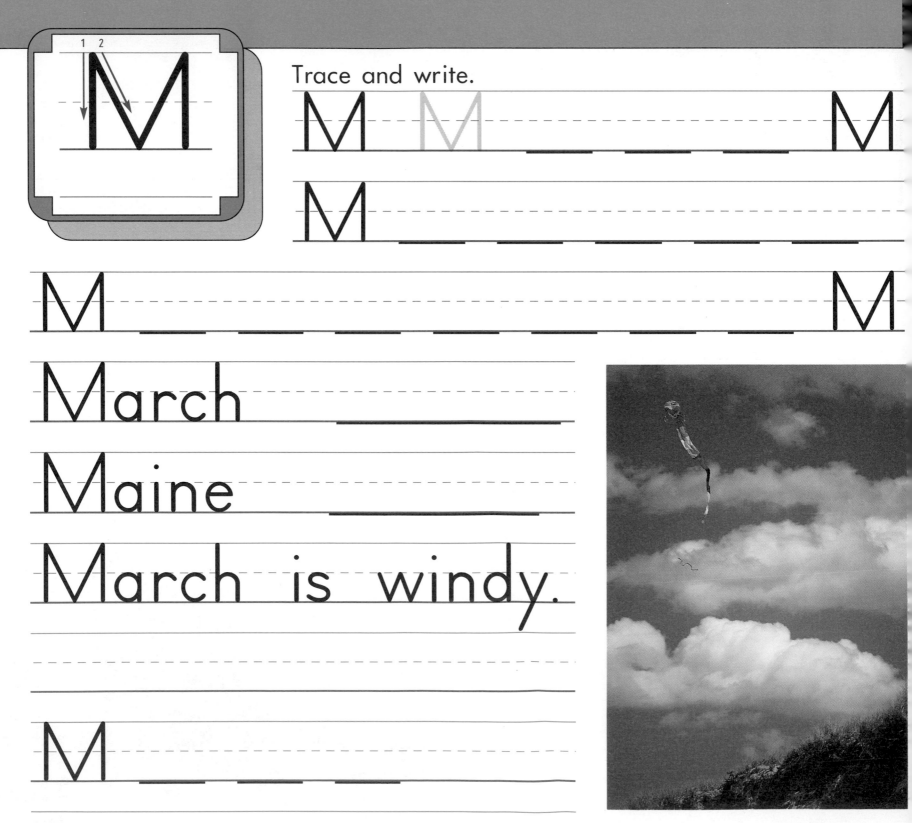

114

May _____

April _____

August _____

November _____

April showers bring May

flowers.

It is sometimes all right to use all uppercase letters.
Write these "things to do" in all uppercase.

SAIL A BOAT

RIDE IN A JEEP

GO ON A BUS TRIP

Write a two-line rhyme about the month in which you were born.

Choose another month and write a two-line poem about it.

Slant Line Letters

Enrichment

My Kite

Cut the paper.
Paste it right.
That's the way
To make a kite.

Unknown

1

2

3

4

5

6

V

V   V   V   V

V

V   V

Valerie thinks the
Velveteen Rabbit is real.

V

Write a story about a
toy that comes to life.

120

W

Trace and write.

W W W W

W

W W

Where the
Wild Things Are

W

Trace and write.

Y   Y   Y   Y

Y

Y   Y

Yell

Yellow

"A Yell for Yellow"

Y

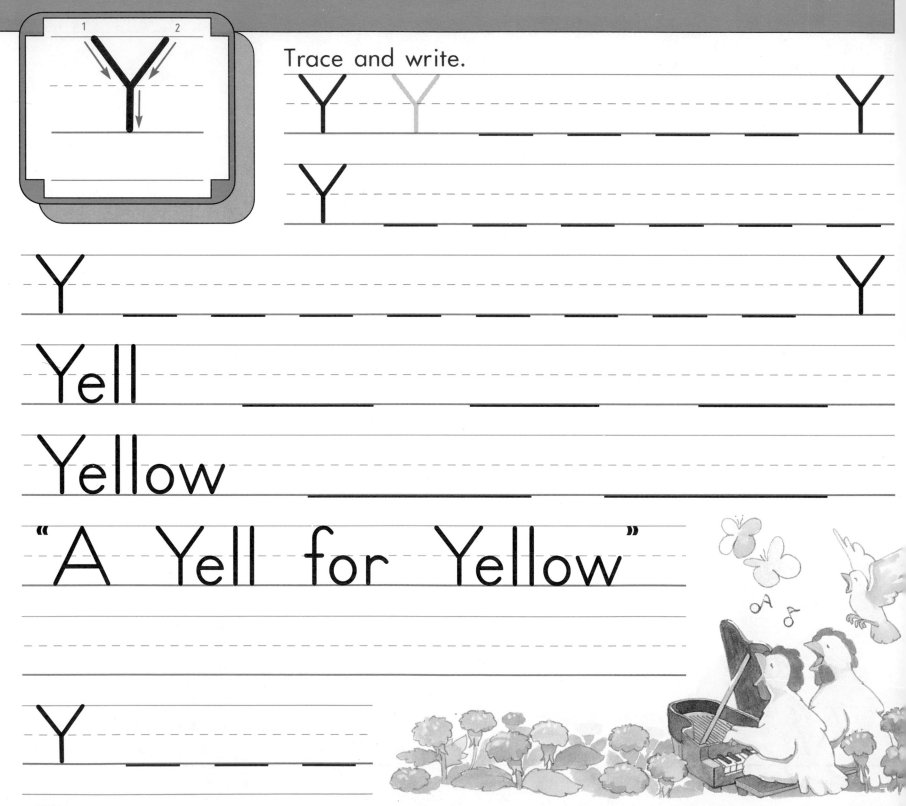

Let's Review

V W Y

Write the letters and words.

V ___ ___ ___ ___ Y ___ ___ ___ ___

W ___ ___ ___ ___ ___ ___ ___ ___

When We Were Very Young

Poem	♥ Table of Contents ♥	Page
Waterlilies		31
Wrong House		65

Trace and write.

K K K _____ K

K

K _____ K

Koko is a gorilla.

Koko loves kittens.

K _____

Write what you would like to know about Koko.

Trace and write.

X X X X

X ....

X X

Xylophones are hit with

little hammers.

X .....

Trace and write.

Z Z Z _ _ _ _ Z

Z _ _ _ _

Z _ _ _ _ Z

Zing go the strings.

Which is largest?

Z _ _ _

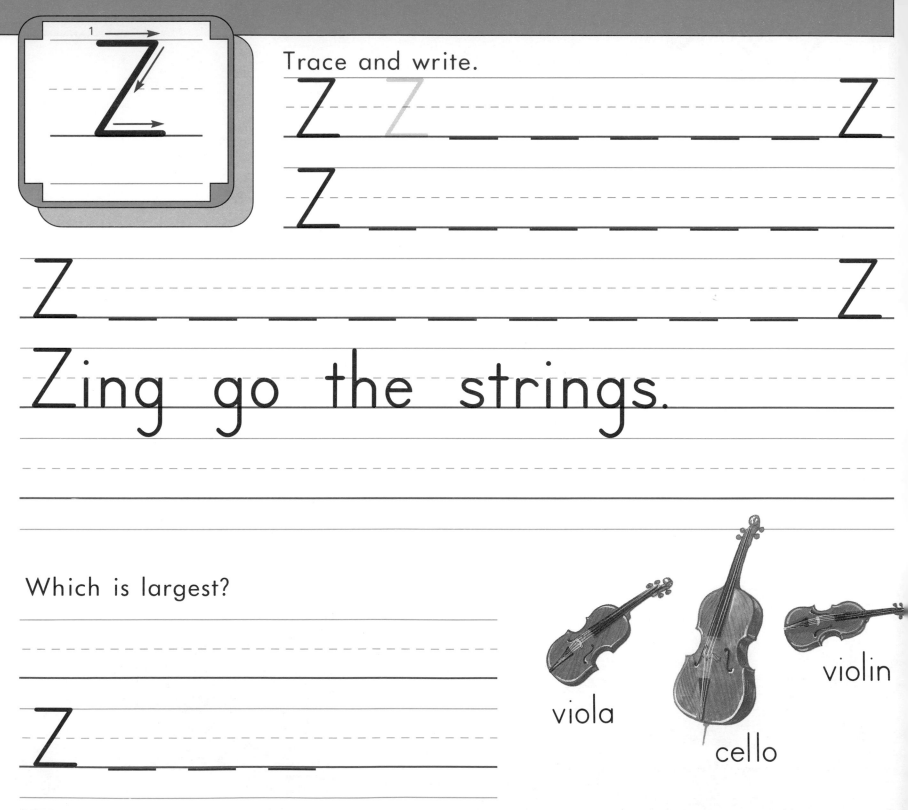

viola

cello

violin

Let's Review

K X Z

Write the sentences below.

1. Keyboards make many sounds.

2. Xylophones are fun.

3. Zithers have many strings.

Checkpoint
Are my lines straight? ☐ Yes ☐ No

Rhymes

The playground is fun.
We like to run.
We slip and slide.
It's fun playing outside.
Susan Mason, Age 7

Write a word that rhymes with each word in the box.

name		light	
cat		top	
play		gold	
run		hill	

Two-Line Rhymes

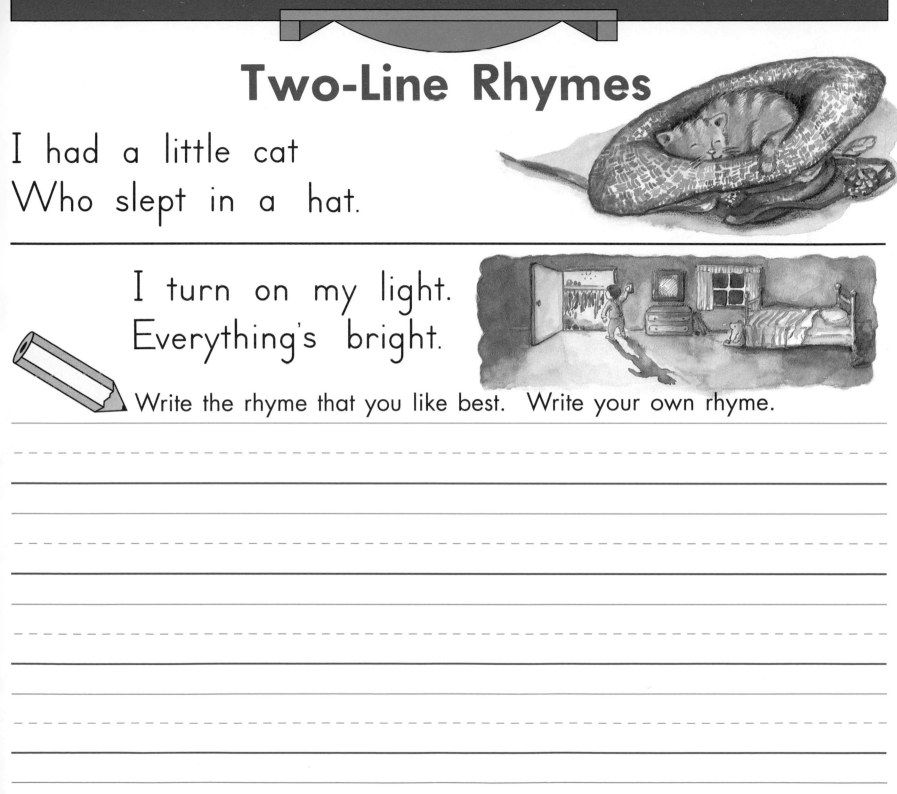

I had a little cat
Who slept in a hat.

I turn on my light.
Everything's bright.

Write the rhyme that you like best.   Write your own rhyme.

ABC Order

Which letters are missing? Write them.

_ a _ c d _ _ g _ i j _ l m _

o _ _ r s t _ v _ _ y _

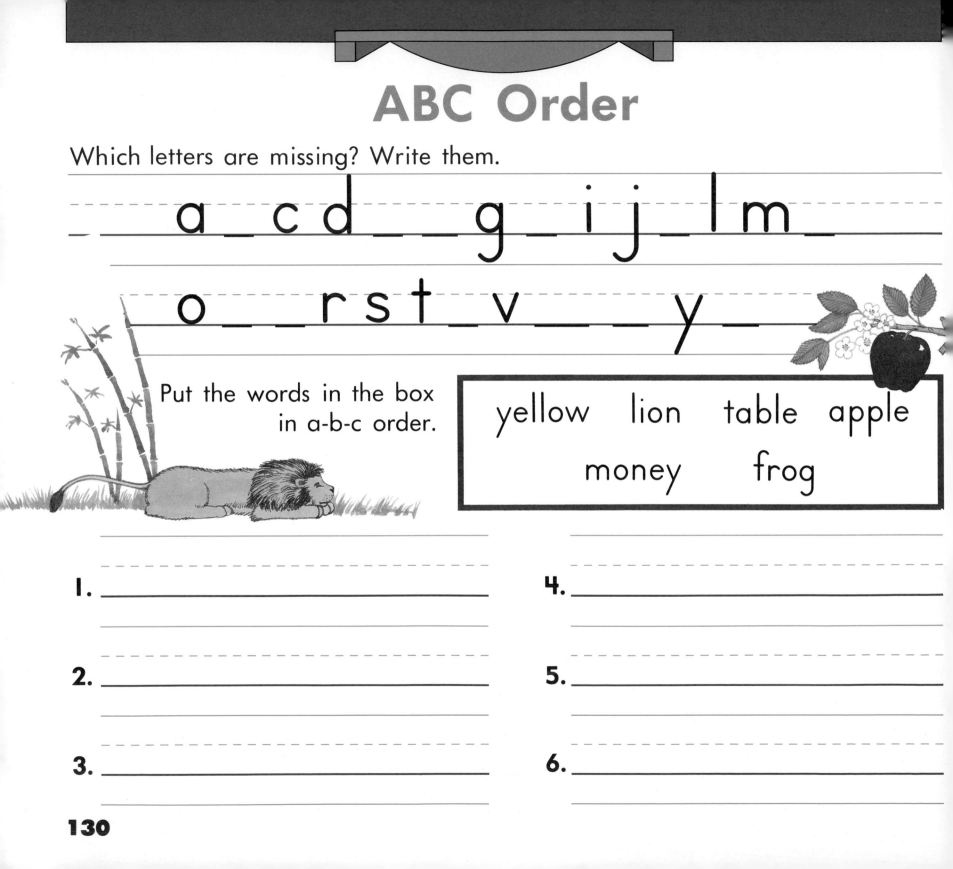

Put the words in the box
in a-b-c order.

yellow	lion	table	apple
	money	frog	

1. _____

2. _____

3. _____

4. _____

5. _____

6. _____

Opposites

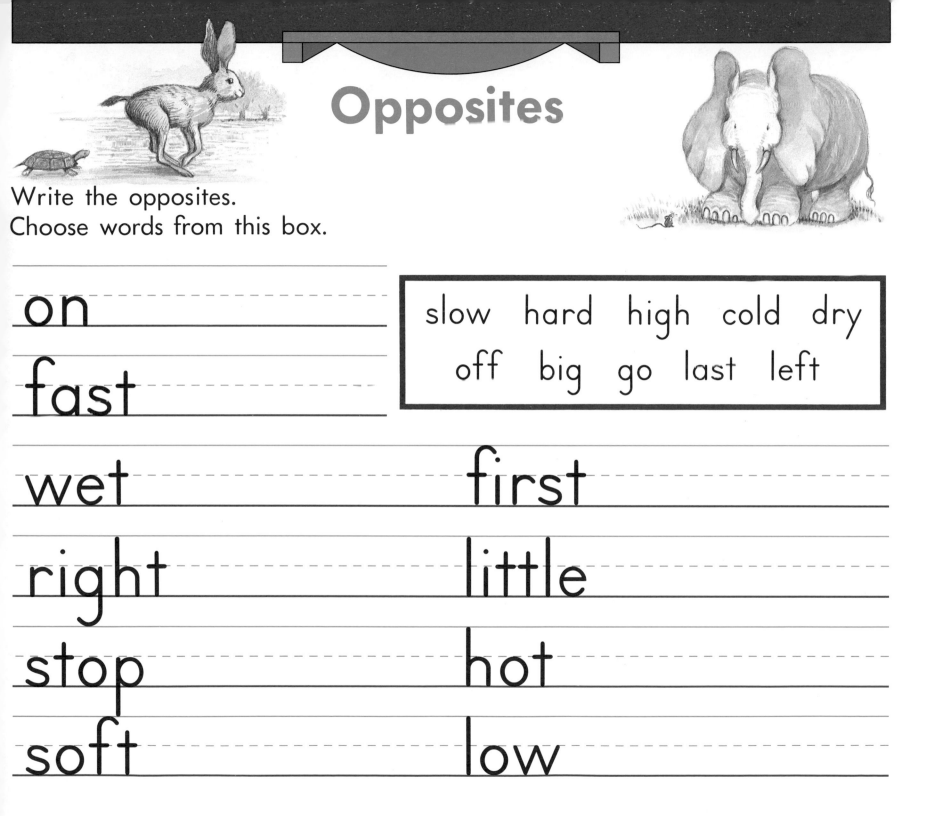

Write the opposites.
Choose words from this box.

slow hard high cold dry	
off big go last left	

on _____

fast _____

wet _____ first _____

right _____ little _____

stop _____ hot _____

soft _____ low _____

Finish the Story

The Surprise

One day Daddy brought home a big box.
It was something for me.
I quickly went over to look inside.

What was in the box? Finish the story.

Write a Poem

Saturday Night

I gave my dog a bath one day.
It was a sight to see!
I got so wet myself, I'd say
He gave the bath to me!

Lois F. Pasley

Write a poem about your pet or a friend.

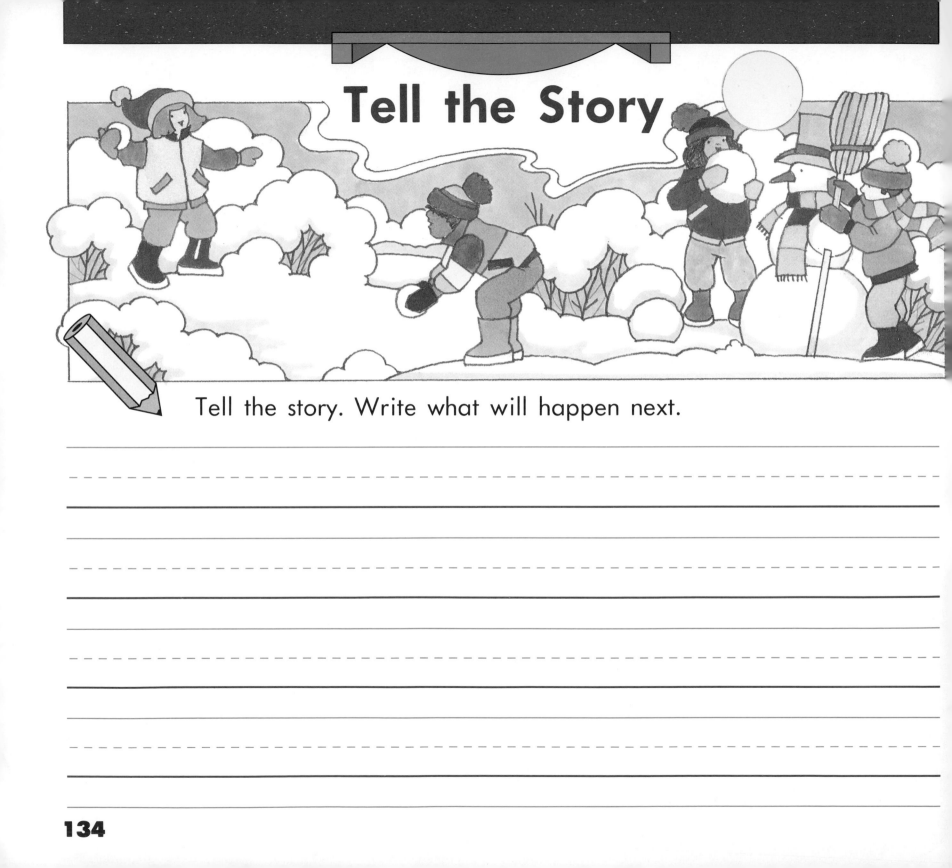

Tell the Story

Tell the story. Write what will happen next.

I Am Special

Write four things you can do.

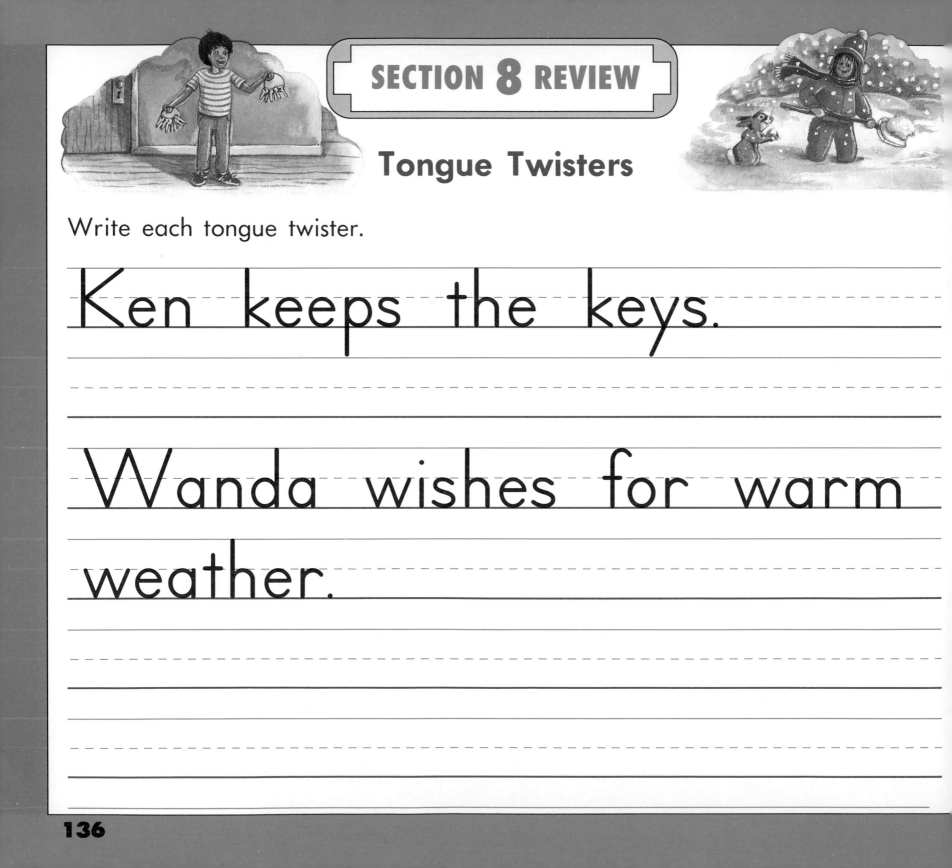

Tongue Twisters

Write each tongue twister.

Ken keeps the keys.

Wanda wishes for warm

weather.

Valerie viewed the village in the valley.

Yes, the yo-yo is yours.

Zoom, zebras, zoom!

Writing a Letter

Dear Aunt Cindy,
    I can't wait to see you on your farm this summer. Can we ride your horse?
    Love,
    Nicholas

Write Nicholas's letter or one of your own.

Summer Fun

Write what you like to do in the summer.

My name is:

My address is:

140

Student Record of Handwriting Skills

Manuscript

	Needs Improvement	Mastery of Skill		Needs Improvement	Mastery of Skill
Writes top to bottom stroke.	☐	☐	Writes the letter **q**.	☐	☐
Positions paper properly.	☐	☐	Writes the letter **u**.	☐	☐
Writes left to right stroke.	☐	☐	Writes the letter **s**.	☐	☐
Holds pencil properly.	☐	☐	Writes the letter **b**.	☐	☐
Writes backward circle.	☐	☐	Writes the question mark.	☐	☐
Writes forward circle.	☐	☐	Writes the letter **p**.	☐	☐
Writes slant right stroke.	☐	☐	Writes the letter **r**.	☐	☐
Writes slant left stroke.	☐	☐	Writes the letter **n**.	☐	☐
Writes the letter **l**.	☐	☐	Writes the exclamation mark.	☐	☐
Writes the letter **i**.	☐	☐	Writes the letter **m**.	☐	☐
Writes the letter **t**.	☐	☐	Writes the letter **h**.	☐	☐
Writes the letter **o**.	☐	☐	Writes the letter **v**.	☐	☐
Writes the period.	☐	☐	Writes the letter **y**.	☐	☐
Writes the letter **a**.	☐	☐	Writes the letter **w**.	☐	☐
Writes the letter **d**.	☐	☐	Writes the letter **k**.	☐	☐
Writes the letter **c**.	☐	☐	Writes the letter **x**.	☐	☐
Writes the letter **e**.	☐	☐	Writes the letter **z**.	☐	☐
Writes the letter **f**.	☐	☐	Writes the numeral **l**.	☐	☐
Writes the letter **g**.	☐	☐	Writes the numeral **2**.	☐	☐
Writes the letter **j**.	☐	☐			

Manuscript

	Needs Improvement	Mastery of Skill
Writes the numeral **3**.	☐	☐
Writes the numeral **4**.	☐	☐
Writes the numeral **5**.	☐	☐
Writes the numeral **6**.	☐	☐
Writes the numeral **7**.	☐	☐
Writes the numeral **8**.	☐	☐
Writes the numeral **9**.	☐	☐
Writes the numeral **10**.	☐	☐
Writes the letter **L**.	☐	☐
Writes the letter **I**.	☐	☐
Writes the quotation marks.	☐	☐
Writes the letter **T**.	☐	☐
Writes the letter **E**.	☐	☐
Writes the letter **F**.	☐	☐
Writes the letter **H**.	☐	☐
Writes the letter **O**.	☐	☐
Writes the letter **Q**.	☐	☐
Writes the comma.	☐	☐
Writes the letter **C**.	☐	☐

	Needs Improvement	Mastery of Skill
Writes the letter **G**.	☐	☐
Writes the apostrophe.	☐	☐
Writes the letter **P**.	☐	☐
Writes the letter **R**.	☐	☐
Writes the letter **B**.	☐	☐
Writes the letter **D**.	☐	☐
Writes the letter **U**.	☐	☐
Writes the letter **S**.	☐	☐
Writes the letter **J**.	☐	☐
Writes the letter **A**.	☐	☐
Writes the letter **N**.	☐	☐
Writes the letter **M**.	☐	☐
Writes the letter **V**.	☐	☐
Writes the letter **W**.	☐	☐
Writes the letter **Y**.	☐	☐
Writes the letter **K**.	☐	☐
Writes the letter **X**.	☐	☐
Writes the letter **Z**.	☐	☐

Good Sitting Position

- Sit comfortably.
- Place both arms on the table with the elbows just off the desk.
- Keep feet flat on the floor.

How to Hold Your Pencil

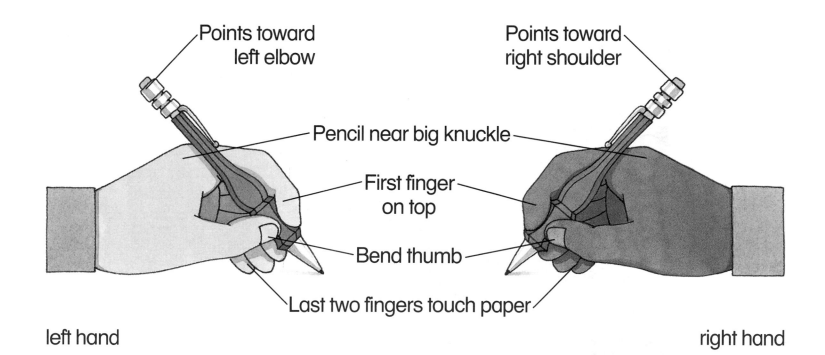

Points toward
left elbow

Points toward
right shoulder

Pencil near big knuckle

First finger
on top

Bend thumb

Last two fingers touch paper

left hand

right hand

Paper Position for Manuscript Writing

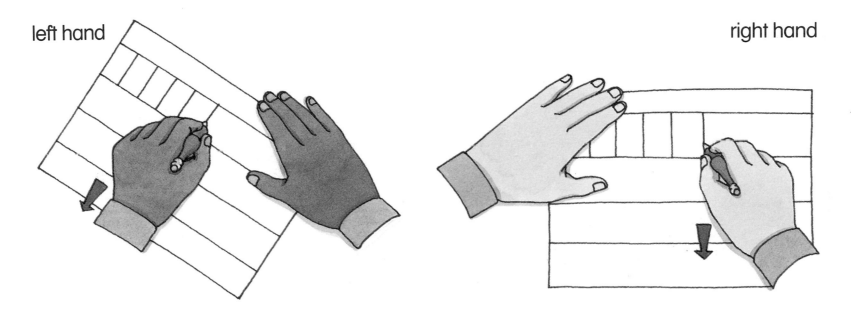

left hand

right hand

Pull
downstrokes
toward the
left elbow.

Pull
downstrokes
toward the
midsection.